FREEDOM'S PURSUIT

THE FUNDAMENTALS

JUAN NAGORE

AltPublish.com

Freedom's Pursuit by Juan Nagore

ISBN: 978-1-7332459-2-0

Publisher: AltPublish.com
Cover Composite Images: Man with hands by Everst, Shutterstock.com / Flag: 123rf.com/Stillfx
Cover design: William Gensburger
Interior images by Juan Nagore unless otherwise indicated.
Distribution of Household Income 2014 graphic reprinted courtesy of US Census Bureau www.census.gov

CONTENTS

DEDICATION

This pursuit, this journey, began a long time ago with ideas and discoveries acquired from my life's experiences and challenges, learned from the ups and downs, the risks and opportunities, all elevated by a lifetime of unexpected blessings. This narrative is but one way to give thanks to all those who shared their thinking, taught me, and created the recognition that life is not easy. Responsibility and risk are not only a challenge to a life, but the foundational experiences that helped me to develop my talents: to apply principle, to never stop thinking in new ways, to never stop learning, and to always give thanks to God and all those who touched me in some special way.

To Mary, for sharing God's gift of love, charity and hope, and, for showing me that the three are all interconnected; one cannot exist without the other. To Angelica, Juan, Sara and Cindy; our present and future became one because of you. You are the blessings in our lives.

To Papa Joe for showing me that kindness resides in our hearts and that to dignify others never goes unnoticed. To Magui who showed me/us what it means to welcome, serve, care and love others; these are the essential gifts of life.

To Richard and Margaret: failure in life's pursuits is not an option, regardless of the risks involved; life is better served with courage and purpose.

To the "Walker" who defined determination and who, with unlimited drive, showed the product of that ultimate pursuit regardless of his disability, and who walks upright with head held high.

To Jim Neihart who showed me what leadership and mentoring are; that success depends on understanding the problem, defining the strategy, and seeking the best solution for all involved.

To Mike Livingston who discussed the questions, argued the issues, and gave form to many of these ideas.

To Paul Cosca who posited new ideas and helped me explore my rational thought.

To the children living in poverty around the world whose lives, liberty and choices are limited and burdened by the circumstances created through warfare, uneducated and ideological leaders, and political corruption.

To the liberals who believe that to achieve life's purpose requires the approval of government; and who see political power and its mechanics as the solution.

To the lessons of the past, and hopes for the future.

To Bill who asked the first question.

There are many others who deserve my thanks for their friendship and who have contributed discourse and ideas, but those listed above are those that have had the most influence and to whom I dedicate this narrative.

~Juan Nagore

FOREWORD

All expression of individual thought requires perspective; and we are guided by it in concert with our life's past experiences. These experiences are reflected in our knowledge and power and revealed in our present circumstance. They reflect our past including its conflicts and opportunities and advance us in the present. Life is the product of all that has preceded us and our futures are dependent upon our perspective and the choices we make, both good and bad. A perspective built upon our singular life experience and impacted by the shared experience and preferences of the broader community. Given this context I am reminded of the opening paragraph of Charles Dickens, *A Tale of Two Cities:*

> *"It was the best of times, it was the worst of times, it was the age of wisdom, it was the age of foolishness, it was the epoch of belief, it was the epoch of incredulity, it was the season of*

> *Light, it was the season of Darkness, it was the spring of hope, it was the winter of despair, we had everything before us, we had nothing before us, we were all going direct to Heaven, we were all going direct the other way – in short, the period was so far like the present period, that some of its noisiest authorities insisted on its being received, for good or for evil, in the superlative degree of comparison only."*

And so it seems today, conflicts are everywhere, friends, work, neighbors, and communities. Each demanding their needs be satisfied while declaring the righteousness of their position, needs that are essential to peace and progress. All defined by individual circumstance and experience.

Our circumstance is the product of our knowledge and power, their application and the subsequent related risks. Our independence is not solely the product of these but they further demand that we think rationally, to reason, in concert with our social and moral beliefs, and act in response to our motivated self-interest. It is this pursuit of opportunity and entrepreneurship which reflects our abilities and shapes our desire to succeed by engaging our humanity at the deepest levels. And in the broader scheme, when combined with other's motivations, they produce a nation's progress.

To have knowledge and to think; this is the greatest gift. No human communication or advancement has ever occurred without knowledge; it is the means by which we speak to each other, to vocalize our needs and our wants. We warn of present danger, seek and undertake risk, and pursue opportunity. We express our dreams in the context of our experience and desires, our success and failures, happiness and joy, and we speak of our love for one another; danger or fear cannot be shared without common knowledge. Knowledge is the source of our decisions and it is the expression of our will, our hopes, aspirations and faith. Without knowledge we remain empty, reacting out of instinct, unable to express feelings or ideas, all of which are expressed through the context of our knowledge and experience. I know who I am, I am aware of my existence, my beliefs, and my world with all its variables including its social competitions, its economic fundamentals, and its political consequences and intrigue.

Knowledge permits us to speak of our ideas, pursuits and actions in the context of our circumstance, and purpose. We express our knowledge and aspirations through the actions we take. And through this knowledge we seek to satisfy our self-interest, make decisions, attempt great deeds, and we assume risk and evaluate its outcome. It is only through this context that we describe our decision making processes and express our abilities, desires and pursuits.

We are motivated "to do" those things that satisfy and advance our standing; to do requires the application of two primary factors which are combined to produce every action. The first is our knowledge, our intelligence and applied experience; this permits us to evaluate our choices and actions in the context of the present and the future and decide which action to take based upon the expected good, risk and reward. We measure the results of our decisions and add this to our knowledge. Second, we apply this knowledge and experience through a process of individual acts of "power." The span of this power is self-defined and the extent of it is the product of our individually applied motivation. We apply our power through our decision making and the actions we take to produce results; without this applied power our knowledge produces little and our failure or lack of success becomes acceptable and readily recognizable.

Knowledge and power reside in each of us. How and when we choose to apply these determines the outcomes of the choices we make and the risks we are willing to take. Some of us apply our power through either the pursuit of individual goodness ("Charity, the only form of extremism acceptable to God." ~Pope Francis); or in the pursuit of creativity, innovation and wealth. For others it lies in the pursuit of political power. Still, many fail to act on this individualized power choosing not to pursue its benefits to either improve circumstance or pursue opportunity; and in the process they defer / grant / shift their power to others who seek it. No risk, no reward.

Knowledge and power describe the creative and analytical processes of our minds, the innovation of our ideas, and the goodness of our actions. They reflect and demonstrate the individual risks we are willing to take. These range from the motivations that transform our lives to the application of ideas which are intended to preserve and extend our power; and, which motivate us to pursue new ideas, good and bad, to some future end.

We apply our knowledge and power to fully understand our politics and what is necessary to achieve economic success. To reach the top one must have opportunity and choice, a choice which isn't hampered but rather is supported by the economic and political system. Human needs are present in all economic and political systems but are only fully satisfied within the political context of freedom. The rules, then, that govern society will ultimately determine whether or not there will be individual growth, freedom, suppression or repression. This combination of knowledge and power in the end is the greatest expression of our freedom; it produces a new and expanded economy and improves the quality of life.

We possess knowledge, risk, a competitive spirit, morals, and the desire for power; and their application in our decisions determines our futures and destinies, individually, socially, economically and politically. Freedom's Pursuit is the combination of all of these ideas which are essential to our desire to advance and contribute to the greater good. Each provides the ability to evaluate and judge rather than subscribe to the agenda of the day. They are the means necessary to protect individuality and to advance society. Knowledge after all is the first step in communication.

INTRODUCTION

This narrative began as a simple quest, a personal pursuit, to answer the question: *What is my world view?* In the process of answering it became a much larger exploration of ideas and individual pursuits including the answer to the original question. To fully answer the question it became necessary to consider much larger issues such as the following points: (1) The application of knowledge to broad issues related to the interactions between people. (2) The combined consequence of knowledge, power, risk and competition; which lead to the most fundamental and consequential of outcomes: Progress. These ideas create social and economic changes by focusing attention on the diverse opportunities and social issues of the day. (3) The challenge of leadership and the subsequent impact on group dynamics, what works and what doesn't. (4) In trying to comprehend the world it was necessary to give context to my own beliefs which required understanding and definition of freedom and purpose, including the impact of morals, mores, philosophy and truth on our decision making. (5) Without this context is any individual able to recognize and respond to those external influences that exert control over us and which impact risk, competition, creativity and investment. (6) Finally, this pursuit was undertaken to discover what it is about me and us and our social interactions that direct our individual destinies and the progress of our culture, communities and nation.

Thus began a quest to find a credible explanation to understand the complexities of social action and speech, the application of knowledge, principles, philosophy, risk, competition, and political speak. Was it possible to reconcile and bring understanding to the American political construct when considering knowledge, power, motivation, and its consequences?

To further understand this perspective I introduced an alternative concept resulting in a paradigm shift of thought from "Worldview" to "Manview" in which individually we accept responsibility for that which is wrong within one's self. And, can this be considered in the context of the human spirit, individuality, rights and freedom of choice. These practices may not be necessarily "rights," nor might they be moral, but they can be acceptable to society as a whole.

To provide context to the definition of Manview consideration was given to the impact of leadership and group dynamics in the marketplace, private and public, and how these parallel a nation's "political" scene; after all, societies evolve and decline through their social and political practices. This, then, is an effort to explain the complexity of the marketplace and the impact of political power on the individual. However, to counter this extraordinary political power it is dependent upon each of us to apply our individual knowledge, pursue our motivated self-interest, and exercise our individual power. It is only through this discovery that political power can be effectively countered.

To understand this "power of the individual" consideration was given to the various elements which are necessary for any society to exist in terms of their own social, economic and political environments. To accomplish this various cities, states and nations were examined and commented upon based on today's competitions. Once these foundations were presented it was essential to consider the interaction of these various elements and their impact on the governance culture. If the forces of knowledge and risk associated with people and economics cannot offset the power of the government then the fundamental idea and understanding of freedom has been lost.

Knowledge and how we apply it or use it to our benefit is the motivation to better understand the broader implications of our social and political interactions. To address this point required the exploration of various ideas: (1) Knowledge and power, these are the product of our education, experience and motivations; (2) Risk, without it progress cannot occur, we consider its cost/price, physical and financial implications on every critical decision; and (3) Truth, its pursuit produces the moral of act of caring for one another, and the associated and obligated mutual protection for each other's well-being regardless of personal risk. At the end of the day is it possible to be a *just* person without knowledge, without understanding the associated risks, and, without seeking truth? Is it possible in the application of these principles to produce a clear vision of our individual purpose?

To address these concepts a hierarchy of human thinking and behavior was created. This considers the ideas of social mores (alternatively: social acceptance), principles, philosophy, morality and truth. To gain a stronger perspective on these elements and their implications the social and political ramifications were further considered to produce a credible definition of freedom. An independence which must be defended through the application of individual knowledge, power and risk and shared communion based upon the pursuits of truth and purpose.

Finally, to fully reach the definition of my world view, or more importantly, my Manview, it was necessary to consider my own education, knowledge, experience and my own personal pursuits. Only after I considered these different elements could I begin to state what I believe. This understanding will hopefully provide the ability to change and to fully apply my Freedom's Pursuit.

As I explored these ideas of my *Freedom's Pursuit,* consideration was applied to existing data, research, and the impact of ideologies. After evaluating these concepts, four fundamental ideas were identified, each differentiated by individual thought and action.

- *Fundamental 1: Knowledge, the Progress Requisite; and, Risk, the Judgment Imperative.*
- *Fundamental 2: The Realities of Power and Competition.*
- *Fundamental 3: Preserving the Requisites for Advancement, Progress, & Opportunity*
- *Fundamental 4: The Constant Pursuit of Excellence and Freedom.*

Each idea explained with the expectation that it is only through understanding these fundamentals can the complexity of life and its circumstance be analyzed to produce effective decision making (ie: applying knowledge to our decisions and behavior; recognizing and granting consideration to those external power factors which influence our lives; and through this recognition evaluate the impact of their related risk.) Through this process we expand and confirm our freedom. Or, in the worst case scenario, we will grant power to others who desperately seek it and which they will gladly take.

The purpose of this narrative is to arrive at a greater understanding of our individual interaction within a complex society, an economic system and an extraordinarily political form of government. Freedom then is the unrestricted expression of our knowledge, risk, competition of ideas, moral perspectives and the choices we make. In the end you and I are only limited by what we choose not to do. It is my hope that by the end of this narrative that you, too, will gain an understanding of what it takes to define your own worldview.

THE QUESTION

In a meeting some years ago a fellow teacher said to me, "I don't know what your worldview is?" It was a great question, one that I may not have been able to answer in its entirety had I been pressed to do so. He had struck a chord with me. The moment passed as the conversation moved on, but the thought of trying to answer this question defining my worldview, stuck with me. What did it mean? Was this a term like "political correctness" that implied you must meet a certain standard defined by, and acceptable to, someone else? After much thought I came up with the following definition: My worldview is a combination of my life's experiences in love, work, faith and, when focused, combined with my education, family, peer involvement, risk, and personal motivations, define who I am and what I believe. My worldview has led me down a path that may have been uncertain at times, but never without interesting twists and turns.

Perhaps a better statement would have been: "That's a conclusion reached without knowing or consideration of the complete facts." We view people and events through our own personal lens of experience and knowledge, based upon our own lives. Our worldview is who we are. However, worldview is a dual definition term used to compliment or detract from an individual without anyone having a clear perspective of its definition, intent, or usage. Interesting! Worldview can also be a trap as you can apply two different perspectives. First, the personal viewpoint: "What do I believe?" Second, the social viewpoint: "What does society think you should believe?" In this context worldview takes on two different meanings and, it depends on the person asking the question. For the inquisitor, it is the broadest and often times the most global of interpretations. For the respondent, it is a vague question subject to interpretation of intent, the answer reflected in what the respondent perceives the inquisitor to mean with limited, or lack of, clarity of understanding to the question's original intent. The presumptive belief is that the respondent will have the same interpretation and definition of the term as the inquisitor. Often times the query is asked in a public venue, and by inference the expectation is that all present will have the same perceived definition; but not necessarily so. It is a term that is also meant to imply something about the individual with whom you disagree by asking a rhetorical question without detail, background or clarity of intent. An effective rhetorical tool when used by a person philosophically opposed to whom the question has been asked. For the respondent there must be a clear and requisite understanding of the question being asked.

A worldview is one's view of the world and it is the result of one's personal interaction(s) within it, and not a view defined by society and built upon the prevailing and accepted social norms. Our worldview forms the basis for each of us to evaluate people and issues—our surroundings and events—through our lens of principle, knowledge, and experience. Through it we apply our principles, judgment, and determine the appropriate response to any given situation.

Does worldview have the same meaning as "respect and dignity" or "the understanding of others?" Our perspectives have great impact on how we understand and view our world however we choose to define it. We apply our knowledge and experience to our everyday lives and interpret events and their outcomes based on self-developed criteria. They define our interactions within our culture, our knowledge of economics and define our politics. Our worldview defines our motivations, it establishes the limits of risk which we are willing to take, and gives depth and meaning to our dreams and aspirations.

Our experiential perspective is critical as we attempt to explore, understand and interpret the chaos of national and world events in the context of our beliefs. Sadly, this can also result in prejudices. As a teacher and as a person involved in business and corporate life, knowledge and experience became ever more important to me in attempting to present information in an honest, unbiased and realistic way—information which evolved as an essential element in the presentment of history, culture, economics, politics, progress and change. It is our individual study of the causes, changes and effects of our individual experience that form our ideas and define our attitudes and interpretations of events and not the simple acceptance of the world as we see and hear it.

Our desire to be independent is a reflection of our beliefs and our efforts to explain and define our personal worldview; a view which pushes back against the impact of social and government intervention. It is our *individual* worldview which creates movement and opposition to the accepted *political* worldview.

Can a government have a worldview?

Worldview is the advocated and promoted consent of the government's position which the citizen is expected to accept and pay for as the resolution to any identified problem, large or small. As adults, acting within society, we look to and grant power to government to solve humanity's common social and economic problems. In the process, government minimizes political upheaval and minimizes any threats to its power; by those elected to office, or merely bureaucratic.

Today, governments around the world provide socialized benefits as a means to advance society with the intent of addressing and solving the problems of poverty, advancing education, and providing equality of opportunity—society's well-being. Government creates these programs as a means to address the very same human and economic problems experienced by the individual citizenry; to provide comfort and serve as a panacea for the issues faced by the governed.

Americans, through their silent consent, have generally accepted these benefits without opposition and will oppose any attempt to remove or deprive the citizen of them in the future. It doesn't matter if these benefits are actually received by the governed, or if they are effective in addressing their intended purpose, an expectation has been created by the political system. When offered, citizens expect these benefits to be permanent, paid for by unknown means, regardless of the system of governance. Ultimately, the availability and efficacy of these programs is determined by the wealth of a nation and the success of the society and individual.

This exchange of individuality for benefit is complicated in today's world of instant communication as it is no longer the individual or legislator that might determine right and wrong; but rather the question of what is "socially acceptable" as the prevailing "right" as defined by society. Stated differently it is the promoted, rationalized, justified and accepted "worldview" which may be defined and coerced by the power of group-think and its ally, government. In today's global political scene this unfortunately includes multi-party and single party systems, and theocratic ideologies which have come to rule modern day societies and nations.

Historically, the poorer the nation the fewer the benefits were delivered, regardless, the demand for government intervention remained. As nations became wealthier, programs were offered to the lower income percentile that addressed a myriad of complex problems. In turn this created an ultimate expectation that these programs would continue throughout a citizen's lifetime. Cuba, for example, is a poverty stricken nation in which wealth belongs to the politically powerful while the average citizen struggles economically. Acceptable? Technically *yes,* as all citizens share the same deprivation.

Even with this standard in place, rich nations argued for and ultimately offered safety net programs that addressed virtually every need since government was viewed as the problem solver/solution provider to this never-ending list of social and economic problems and demands. In post-World War II Europe, everything was in short supply: food, housing, healthcare, all were in high demand. Once these benefits—be it a life necessity or tax benefit—was established, the desire for continuing bureaucratic intervention expanded to virtually every income segment of society. As a result, in European countries the average tax today is approximately 50 percent of personal income, combined with an oppressive regulatory system, yet it provides some semblance of shared burden. Shared well-being, not individual success, was, and is, the dominant think—a past historical necessity and a present day political and economic burden leveraged against the common tax payer.

This dependence on government programs is in contrast to nations that support or promote individual independence. In those nations, a greater entrepreneurial drive is expected, and fewer well-being socialized benefits are demanded—the success of the individual defined the future. This entrepreneurial policy creates new ideas and industries, demanding new schools and widespread education systems.

In *"Civil Disobedience,"* Henry David Thoreau asked the question regarding conscience, "Must the citizen ever for a moment resign his conscience to the legislator?" In his question Thoreau asks do we defer, or supplant, our individual motivations, knowledge and responsibilities to each other in exchange for the leadership, protection and benefit derived from government; its decision making and approval. If so, what is it that we have given up, what motivations have we abandoned or deferred, and what have we deprived future generations of? Or, in the absence of freedom, have we given up the right to think and act? Have those in power relegated the individual to a poverty bereft of opportunity, perpetrated by an abuse of power and in which the only option is to flee present circumstance.

. . .

In England, Prime Minister Margaret Thatcher (1979-1990,) led the movement to transform the economy by redefining the government's role, moving the nation from limited growth to economic expansion. She privatized public housing and transportation, addressed coal mining and industrial strikes, and ended low manufactured goods production by closing unprofitable government owned or controlled English companies which were supported and sustained by public money. In doing so she reduced the tax payer burden, reduced regulation, and reconstructed and stimulated the economy based on supply and demand, and, in the end, re-ignited England's entrepreneurial spirit.

Police cars, below their city seals often have the words "to serve and protect." One can consider the idea of "to serve" as a perspective on our attitudes towards humanity—to be kind and charitable; "to protect" us not only from danger, but also from those that would violate our natural rights, civil rights and civil liberties. This is the original definition and understanding of *"equal"* by the founders of America, as stated in the *Declaration of Independence*. Shouldn't this be the goal of each and every citizen? To protect not only our own natural rights, but those of our fellow citizens.

Sadly this statement of "to serve and protect" can also have a political translation meaning that the government has the power to create, grant and apply a new definition of *"equal."* This application of power has caused an evolutionary shift in the definition of freedom that counters that which our public servants were originally sworn to protect—the power of the individual to act in such manner that serves his best interest without causing harm to others. In this revision of "equal" to "equality," the mutual protection provided by citizens is altered to the legislated benefit of one citizen's benefit provided by another. I remain free to choose but with greater restrictions and at a higher price; a power imposed on the citizen by government rather than the individual enjoyment and shared mutual benefits derived from the equality of pursuits and freedom.

Societies advance or decline based upon the active Manview of each citizen and not the worldview of special interests and government. Today, every citizen possesses risk against the unlimited power of the state. Thus, the obligation of the free citizen to be ever vigilant against the power of the state becomes more important as each citizen is not only responsible for his own freedom but also the defense of all citizens. It is through this active process that opportunity is advanced, and subject to these decisions, society creates its blended, positive or negative, worldview of the nation.

PART I

THE FUNDAMENTALS

ESSENTIAL # 1: KNOWLEDGE, THE PROGRESS REQUISITE; RISK, THE JUDGEMENT IMPERATIVE

1

IN CONSIDERATION OF ACQUIRED KNOWLEDGE:

KNOWLEDGE IS THE KEY TO SUCCESS

In 1998 I was working for Enron's subsidiary, Portland General Electric (PGE). Ken Lay, then Chairman and CEO of Enron, came to Portland and announced that after owning the utility for just two years the decision had been made that PGE no longer fit Enron's business model and that Enron was seeking a new owner for the company. Combined with the announcement Lay announced that all future employees would be recruited solely from select colleges and universities from across the country. Among these were MIT, Rice University, University of Texas, Princeton, Harvard and Stanford Universities. And, the basis for the recruitment of any future employee, and/or the pursuit of any future endeavor, would be based on the individual and their creative "intellectual capital," more importantly their contribution to future projects and the overall success of the company.

From 1996 to 2001 Enron was proclaimed by Fortune Magazine as the most "Innovative Company in America" and one of the top 100 companies in the nation to work for (2001); and its stock price growth reflected it. Enron was a self-defined "Market Maker." As such the number one priority for all yet-to-be identified, future projects and acquisitions would be the product of these newly created market opportunities. As a market maker its products had great future potential; relying upon the acceptance of new energy management products by its customers, it moved into new market segments with refined, creative financial and energy products. Enron's growth strategy not only relied upon its ability to create new products, but also from its ability to deliver on its products and promises while serving an ever-expanding group of energy consumers.

However, its new products and its future market potential failed, when it was discovered that its corporate finances, and many of its project finances, were fraudulently reported. The company debt far outstripped its ability to service it. In addition, Enron manipulated California's electric transmission line system controlling the delivery of electric energy to this expanding and demanding market. As a result energy prices soared bringing California close to repeated brownouts, this in a state that had just passed energy deregulation two years before in order to improve the availability of electric energy. This manipulation caused Pacific Gas & Electric Company to file for bankruptcy protection in 2001 and brought Enron under intensive State and Federal review with subsequent criminal charges and senior level managers sent to prison.

The idea of applied intellectual capital is not a new one, but perhaps not as well demonstrated, nor as well executed, as Ken Lay had prognosticated, or its misuse so egregiously applied.

We have always known that the key to success relies upon the continuation and expansion of knowledge and its development. When combined with entrepreneurship and a willingness to pursue risk, knowledge creates new ideas and products. America has an entire system dedicated to this purpose. According to the National High School Center there were 18,435 high schools in America in 2012, serving over 15,000,000 students. There are 4,140 colleges in America offering a dizzying array of accredited courses and degrees to more than 17,500,000 students. Complimenting these facts and demonstrating the change in the pursuit of knowledge, over 57 percent of today's college enrollees are women. We are witnessing a dramatic shift in America's education system, its accessibility, its beneficiaries and its ideological transformative power.

With all this opportunity America remains in seventeenth place in literacy, twentieth place in science, twenty-seventh place in math, and twenty-fourth place in problem solving, according to the Organization for Economic Cooperation and Development (OECD), Program for International Student Assessment (PISA). These numbers reflect America's position vis-à-vis the top 30 nations in the world, as reported in 2012.

The numbers, while not very positive for America, are in their totality perhaps a bit suspect; America is a land of immigrants and continues to be so. We educate everyone and require a minimum of a high school education, equalized by law and national standards. Our numbers are not fully differentiated nor adjusted for cultural experience, expectations and language. As such questions remain, and their answers may speak volumes, about national differences. I wonder whether other countries report the results for all students? Do they have the same national mandate that all students must complete high school? Do they differentiate between those that are college bound versus those that are sent to vocational technical schools? And, if so, are they measured on the same basis?

Anecdotally I spoke to a German college student several years ago and he told me that in Germany students are reviewed for their educational potential in the 9th, 11th and 13th Grades, and their advancement in education is based on this evaluation. In the ninth grade, if your potential to proceed isn't demonstrated, then your education is complete. You become part of the semi-skilled labor force and receive additional work related education. In the 11th Grade, if you are not chosen to advance then you are given the chance to enroll in a vocational school. In the 13th Grade you are again evaluated to determine your potential to continue through college. If you are chosen to continue you advance to college, if not you are given the choice of enrolling in a technical school. If America tests every enrolled student through the 11th Grade, has Germany done the same? Or has it culled out lower performing students raising the nation's overall education performance scores?

The application of knowledge in a free market produces new ideas and products. It is the application of work in science that creates new technologies which in turn leads to new discoveries and new products. This results in new job opportunities throughout the production chain. However, the process of acquired knowledge produces multiple and separate types of work —knowledge based, skilled and unskilled. Depending on an individual's objectives, opportunities and motivation, people seek out the level of knowledge and skills which most satisfies them. For example, a culinary chef creates a unique meal for a guest; the guest looks forward to the experience regardless of price. This experience is distinct from the worker at a fast-food restaurant whose job it is to produce the same meal repeatedly with consistency of taste and form, satisfying a particular consumer, at a consistently low price. We distinguish between these two based on price and our desired level of satisfaction; we evaluate these based on our ability to purchase either alternative. Acquired knowledge produces differentiated outcomes.

Knowledge is involved in the creation of *new* technologies in medicine, research, science, materials, etc. Its application is as diverse as that of doctors, lawyers, engineers, architects and astronomers. Skill-based work encompasses the greatest number of jobs, but it is the most threatened in today's labor market and economy—some jobs may be salaried, others hourly and still others job/contract based. Jobs such as assembly line workers, bankers, mechanics, craftsmen all deal with skill sets which are essential to the production of goods and services, but many jobs can be, or are being, replaced with near-skills at lower wages, supplanted with technological tools and artificial intelligence (AI).

America has historically viewed education as the key to individual success. For today and into the near future this fundamental belief remains. The challenge for America is: Are we meeting the expectations of America's labor market and its future needs? America's labor force is robust, but its ability to be absorbed in productive labor is challenged today as historically high wage skilled jobs seem to have leveled off; and in some instances, are now in decline. America's global businesses are now able to find competitive skills in foreign lands at a percentage of the cost. According to Thomas Friedman, *The World is Flat,* as the global economy takes root and skills are developed around the world, the basic skills of human labor become ubiquitous. Today's growth-winning nations are those that provide not only the skills at a lower or competitive cost, but also the complimentary political and social stability supported by competitive taxes and a pro-growth regulatory environment, all desired by the economic motivators of business.

In America, as Ken Lay prognosticated, intellectual capital has become the objective of both business and politics. Today we seek leaders who possess intellectual capital in both realms and by doing so companies, and the nation, are willing to vest great power and authority in those with this acquired knowledge. The measure of a man or woman today is often based upon his or her education; the higher the education degree the greater the presumption of the person's ability to perform and lead. And yet, as we look at America's past it wasn't an absolute of education; but rather the combination of knowledge, inventiveness, experience, leadership, competition and risk that achieved and created new industry; and, the subsequent employment opportunities provided to an expanding labor force. In a competitive world this combination seems to be on the decline with large companies growing through the acquisition of smaller inventive business niche suppliers and competitors. This fact has been demonstrated by the consolidation of the banking industry over the past 30 years, and the continuing mergers of high tech and bio-tech companies. For example the Roche Corporation has been a major shareholder in America's Genentech since 1990 and acquired full ownership in it as reported by Andrew Pollack in The New York Times, World Business, March 12, 2009.

Acquired knowledge is the gateway by which Americans, in this modern competitive world, advance and achieve, and through it, gain power and position. And, based upon their individual achievement wield great power in business and politics. In business the outcome can be—although not guaranteed—great wealth. This wealth is often acquired through astute management, acquisition, investment and leadership. Thomas Watson of IBM, Bill Gates of Microsoft, Steve Jobs of Apple, Jamie Dimon of JP Morgan Chase, Alan Mulally of Ford, Elon Musk of Tesla and Jeff Bezos of Amazon, all applied acquired knowledge but combined it with industry experience, vision, leadership and risk to create great companies. These men, with a product and world market perspective, focused their companies and developed markets for their products, and, indirectly challenged and forced their competitors to innovate. The outcome: industry leadership and creative products which are accepted worldwide.

Politically we take the idea of acquired knowledge, particularly as it applies to the study of law, and presume that attorneys will make the best politicians and leaders, after all they know and understand the law, and by extension the Constitution. In reality as lawyers they specialize and may have little knowledge of the economy and the diverse population that makes up America's social structures. America elects local politicians, governors, senators, representatives and presidents based on this very idea of acquired knowledge, with the assumption that they will become great American leaders.

In the political world the outcomes can be very different, based on ideology and the resources of government; leadership is driven not by the creation of product but by the delivery of benefit to the electorate. Power is derived by position rather than the creation of product, jobs and wealth. With position comes the ability to propose, pass and create new legislation which benefits voters and special interests, but can hinder the economy and reduce the probability of individual success.

Once in power, through the passage of legislation, benefits and exceptions are created for the electorate and special interests. This process becomes the measure of a politician's effectiveness; did he or she keep their political campaign promises? If yes, are they worthy of re-election? If the passage of legislation is the measurement then no service or benefit provided by government is too small to create political opportunity and power. A politician's electability is measured by his ability to deliver on promises to constituents and special interests. A politician's Worldview then is shaped by his need and ability to be re-elected.

This political process can be combined with the simple desire to do, to do those things that are at the very nature of man, to produce, to create. However, in government the process of creation results in regulations, some good some not. Case in point, I attended a City of Walnut Creek Design Review Commission meeting several years ago, on their agenda was the final approval for an expansion of a Synagogue, a new hall was being added to serve the needs of its members and the community. The Commission began by complimenting the architects and Temple leaders on the creative good design of the facility, and then the "buts" began. The committee felt that more trees and brush needed to be planted near the parking lot. The synagogue's representatives stated that they understood the Commission's request and that they had had trees and bushes there in the past, but with the provision of child care at the site there was a great danger posed to children during the drop off and pick up times. A child could be hidden by the very plants that the commissioners wanted. The commission members said they understood, but that they really wanted the addition of more trees and bushes to the site. The temple's leaders and architects said they understood and would do their best to see what could be done to add more trees and plants as requested.

The commissioners then proceeded to comment on a Pepper tree at the back of the site that would be removed by the expansion. The Synagogue's leaders explained that they were removing the tree at the request of the fire department to provide greater access for emergency vehicles. The commissioners again said they understood, but that they really wanted to keep the tree. The leaders said they would again go back and determine what else could be done.

They then complimented the architects again and asked about the color of the expansion? The community's leaders said it would be alabaster, one commissioner after another stated they were not thrilled with the color alabaster. The leaders in response said they would work with the architect and again see what could be done.

The cost to the synagogue in time and money created by an appointed, non-elected, non-staff, commission wielding power on the basis of desire rather than need has become symbolic of the American political system. It creates laws and regulations for the purpose of achieving desired outcomes. The objective is: If I have a position and I am given responsibility then I must be good at what I do. I must provide the best outcome regardless of cost to whoever is being judged, after all the cost itself is being born by someone else and the risk to government, its politicians, commissions and staff is little to non-existent.

Since listening to the above I learned that the synagogue's project was cancelled; one can only assume that cost considerations were made and the project ended.

The impact of government programs on the social and

economic environments is well intended but often-times misapplied when the application of power is added to the mix. Government's impact, when measured in terms of power, comes at great expense to society as all costs are borne by the tax paying citizen. This is especially true in the absence of any opposing, competitive, counter position. When the use of power is considered, government's impact on society as a whole can be positive or negative in the short term—five years or less—or in the worst scenario, destructive. Any benefit granted by government can be reduced, broadened, modified or even deleted consistent with the needs of the nation and the politics of the day. An example of this is the Affordable Healthcare Act—Obamacare. All actions of governments are a function of the power owned and controlled by the politicians. Any benefit can be created, granted and made permanent regardless of cost; financial accountability is not a measurement of government efficiency. These outcomes are measured against the perceived need and the desired political objective, not the great cost and "risk" to the tax paying citizen.

This, then, raises the question of conscience and the application of principle. This idea is at the very heart of a representative government. By its nature, doing what is right is the fundamental idea of a representative government, with its approval dependent upon the consent of the governed; a consent which the governed accept responsibility for. However, it is difficult to apply principles given the many complex political processes and individual philosophies that exist, conditions, which if not overseen, lead to the creation of moral hazards with citizens obligated to pay for any and all efforts prescribed by the politician. So every citizen and voter must ask the questions: Is the politician acting to address a community need? Is he or she exercising their desire for change and power based on ideology? Or, is it the consequence of influence exerted by special interests arguing for a particular outcome; a sold and justified decision consistent with an ideological agenda, which may go counter to the greater good of every citizen.

Knowledge and Power: Both are competing and leveraged interests essential to the advancement of the individual and the nation. However, to be effective they require a competition of ideas and a willingness to assume risk; each is essential to create success. Without competition and risk knowledge produces limited results. Without knowledge and risk bureaucracies flourish, knowledge flounders and citizens lose. Knowledge by itself isn't power, but it is the key to success.

2

THE INDIVIDUAL AND DISCOVERY

DOES KNOWLEDGE EQUAL FREEDOM?

Knowledge does not produce discovery on its own.

Discovery does not advance a society on its own.

Knowledge can create power.

Knowledge and discovery do not create freedom without risk.

Freedom unless protected from power, will not support the advancement of knowledge.

Education, Knowledge and Opportunity

Every discovery, philosophy or advancement, whether, technical or social, has had its origins in the actions of a single individual who saw a wrong, had a new idea, or saw an opportunity. Every social evolution has been the result of individual action or a movement initiated by a single person which culminated in a new direction impacting millions of other people. Sometimes these social movements turned out for the worse creating oppression and limiting opportunity, and for many, progress. Any discussion regarding worldview or freedom, must begin with the question of the individual and his or her ability to seek the highest and best opportunity given present and future conditions, within their social, economic and political realms.

Personal pursuits are defined by the knowledge and freedom each person possesses. This is either supported or suppressed by the culture, the educational system, economic creativity and opportunity; or the political system in place. To achieve change and/or success requires that there be a perfect storm in which these factors interact in a positive way, supporting not suppressing the individual in his endeavors. Any one factor alone can negatively impact the others and limit an individual's personal opportunity.

Discovery is then defined as a personal triumph of thoughtful contemplation, knowledge, intellectual pursuit, creativity, problem solving and individual determination. Effective discovery can happen when supported or paid for by government, the Apollo moon landing and cancer research for example. However in the greater marketplace, it is the application of knowledge and market-driven ideas which produce higher order thinking leading to innovation. To advance discovery an economy must have access to risk capital (money), and must be protected from excessive government power, regulation and entanglements. Limited and regulated governmental power supports the greater good and increases the probability of transforming a society and an economy thus advancing social opportunity. To succeed a society must protect itself from the competing and complimentary power of corruption; a power which can exist at all levels of government and business and drains the society of its natural desire for knowledge and discovery. Examples abound and can be found around the world in which individuals and institutions see other people's money as a way to advance and enrich themselves.

<u>The Complete Thinker</u>

> *"Complete thinking means grasping the hierarchy of knowledge, that is, thinking important thoughts, the most important thoughts, the highest and best thoughts. From this elevated perspective, as it were, we see how everything else fits together.*
>
> *"Complete thinking means thinking worthwhile thoughts that are literally worth our time – the most limited commodity that we have. Thinking should not be a waste of time. It should be the most productive and fruitful use of our time, leading to worthwhile actions that reflect our thinking.*
>
> *"Critical thinking means knowing how to fill in the blanks, that is, how to fill the gaps in our knowledge. We cannot know everything, but we can connect what we do know with coherence."*
>
> *~Dale Ahlquist, The Complete Thinker, page 18 & 19*

The more individuals who have access to education, the greater the probability of national economic success. But education isn't automatic. If parents demand, society expects, and a nation mandates, then the power to learn, along with social advancement, is born. If knowledge is restricted by money, cultural behavior, government limitations, religious ideology or gender, then the opposite occurs. If the education system is the means for teaching political thought and indoctrination, then the outcome is predictable. If the education system creates and provides only the knowledge which is required to serve the needs of the state and not the advancement of the individual and society, then the outcome is again predictable. The more educational opportunities and choices provided to the individual and all citizens by the system of governance the greater the society's creativity, and by extension, the greater the potential for social and economic advancement.

Education advances and redefines the status quo by altering the very basic wants and needs of every individual as well as society in general, regardless of location. The better, the more diverse and complex the education system, the more advanced the society; and by extension, the more advanced their economic condition. Education based on the pursuit of knowledge permits the advancement of every nation.

Knowledge is a personal pursuit and opportunity creator. Without opportunity discovery is limited and the ignitor of social improvement restrained; the status quo is preserved. Discovery, then, exists in two forms: the first, scientific discovery, the result of slow meticulous research (the polio vaccine, cancer research and new drugs, space exploration, etc); the second, market gap discovery, when an opportunity is identified within an existing developing market (John D. Rockefeller (Exxon-Mobil), Henry Ford (Ford Auto.), Andrew Carnegie (American Steel Co.'s), Bill Gates (Microsoft), Steve Jobs (Apple) and Mark Zuckerberg (Facebook)).

Creativity, knowledge and productivity are easily reflected in new discoveries and the subsequent number of patents filed with and granted by individual nations, or the World Intellectual Property Organization, to individuals and corporations, is a basic measurement of creativity. As can be seen in the following chart creativity is not only reflected in the quantity of patents requested but also more importantly the quantity approved. Furthermore, patent filings are an indirect descriptor of a nation's scientific and productive output, a demonstration of a nation's educational foundation which advances and reflects a nation's entrepreneurial opportunities and priorities. In the following table, for example, China leads in applications but falls behind the United States and Japan in patents granted.

Patent Applications in 2011 By Office, in '000

Source: World Intellectual Property Organization

Nation	Patent Applications ('000's	Patents Granted
China	525	172
United States	500	225
Japan	340	238
South Korea	175	95
European Patent Office	140	62

A second way to look at a nation's progress is to look at its college enrollment. College enrollment is a further reflection of a society's priorities and beliefs in the power of the individual. No modern society can operate, nor compete, without the advancement of the individual; societies that don't seek the advancement of the individual tend to have centralized power and are weak economically resulting in limited education and fewer economic opportunities. These nations are incapable, or unwilling, to fund advanced public education. When wealth is concentrated in the hands of the privileged and the corrupt, their agendas result in reduced national investment in education. This is further complicated by the intent of the wealthy to protect personal wealth; they export their dollars to safer harbors depriving the nation and citizenry of the necessary investments in education and knowledge-based creativity. This becomes a lost future founded on a non-expanding economy and lost opportunity.

Nation	Percent of Young Adults Enrolled in College	Percent of Population with High School Equivalency Ages 25 – 64 in the 2017
S. Korea	53	88
Belgium	37	77
United States	34	91
France	31	78
Canada	30	91
Germany	25	87
United Kingdom	22	81
Mexico	14	38

The combinations of these various approaches to the application and expansion of knowledge provides insight into the priorities of nations and societies. Without knowledge societies can't advance; these societies lose ground in the competitive global economy to nations in which knowledge is developed, applied and shared among all citizens. More importantly, knowledge stands out as the critical component demonstrating the degree to which freedom advances in any nation. When citizens have knowledge, information is analyzed and applied, people create, take individual risk, and nations advance.

3

RISK

INNOVATION DESTROYS THE STATUS QUO

When knowledge is applied one of the major outcomes is entrepreneurship, it is the natural by-product of knowledge. The entrepreneurial application of this knowledge however requires that an individual take "Risk." Today, no modern society can function well without risk; it is the means by which innovation occurs, products invented, technological advancements made, wealth created, and ultimately, quality of life improved.

We historically associate risk with the potential loss of money or personal harm, but rarely is "Risk" considered as an element of Social Change. And yet, every society has evolved as a consequence of individuals taking great personal risk when the need for change arose; a process created and carried out through either mass protest against existing oppressions, the American Civil Rights Movement, or revolution against existing political structures, the present day protests against the Maduro regime in Venezuela.

Social change comes at great expense to individual life and livelihood as risks are taken to pursue and achieve desired political and social change. In the pursuit of political change men and women have and are willing to risk life and well-being to achieve a higher level of personal, economic and political freedom. Consider the American Revolution, the American Civil War or more recently the revolts in the Middle East (Egypt, Libya and Syria), and the current migration of Arabs from Syria to Western Europe. The outcome may not have been what was originally envisioned but none-the-less change occurred.

Information is the basis for developing, measuring and evaluating opportunity and risk, without this application of knowledge we cannot move beyond the present. Risk, in one form or another, is at the heart of every decision and action. We evaluate circumstances and conditions based on our risk tolerance. To determine this we apply our knowledge and experience to both individual and economic conditions, we pursue personal and professional advancement, investments, relationships, purchases and safety based on this evaluation of risk and circumstance.

Personal Risk is at the center of all change. Personal Risk exposes the individual to the possibility of losing everything that constitutes the person including his life.

When you consider risk and apply it to the political, social and economic environments of modern societies, *risk* is present in only the social and economic sectors. The political realm, and bureaucracies, hold no risk; all risk is transferred to, or owned by, the people and businesses within the nation by virtue of citizenship and membership in the economy.

In the pursuit of change or wealth *economic risk* entails the possible loss of everything of value in the pursuit of a future desired outcome. Economic analysis shows that when new jobs are created there is a direct impact on the health and vitality of a community and all market segments. Risk is measured in different ways here, but primarily in market risk, financial gain or loss. A person can lose the means of work, income and property, or conversely, gain wealth if properly pursued and managed. If this is a gain, then all is well, however, if this is a loss, then the greater the loss the more challenged the recovery.

If an individual chooses to undertake risk in an attempt to advance personal, economic or political change, and loses, the only thing that isn't lost is the individual's knowledge and experience; these are imbedded in his very nature and persona and will serve to aid him in his recovery to do battle another day.

However, consider workers who have been laid off as a result of corporate downsizing, recession or outsourcing, as they search and find new jobs they soon discover that the new replacement job rarely pays the equivalent, or greater income, than the job previously held. Today, those who have lost good paying jobs may also have lost homes and other assets of value in the process, moving into a future which not only pays less but also produces a probable reduction in their future standard of living and opportunity.

Under these circumstances many individuals find themselves having to restart careers, rebuild personal skills and re-establish a new financial base. This process can include attempts to replace lost property, lost wealth and rebuild their standard of living at a potentially lower income level. It is for this reason that pursuing employment change is better done while employed; the individual is better positioned to trade on current skillsets and income to improve future earnings.

What about the wealthy, do they possess risk or do they

possess power? The wealthy may have gained wealth from a variety of sources. Regardless, their personal financial risk is diminished as long as they manage their assets well in both the near and long term. Do the wealthy possess power? Yes, but only within their sphere of influence—their companies, immediate social circles, and their communities. A wealthy individual may contribute money to political causes, but their money doesn't provide consistent, derived power outcomes. Money, in economic terms, has temporary or transitional power, reflected only in the winning outcomes of the issues they support. To benefit from economic power a wealthy person's beliefs must be in concert with a special interest group's political objectives, essential to the justification for monetary support and contributions. At the end of the day this may be the extent of their political involvement. Consider Tom Steyer, a California billionaire, who has been on a personal mission to impeach President Trump. While his cause has great appeal to certain segments of the electorate, as of this writing Congress has only voted to proceed with an investigation into the actions of the President which could lead to impeachment. To elevate his cause he decided to become a presidential candidate and has entered the already crowded Democratic field.

Money buys limited and temporary power within the political organizations they agreed to support, with little or no personal risk. Money is the active voice for individuals, labor unions and social movements. It buys influence, and it advances political agendas. If their cause loses an election, then their effort at buying influence has only produced visibility for the cause, but no real personal power. The rich, unions and special interests, can promote their political beliefs. Real power then remains solely the domain of government; it transfers risk to the citizen, and it can choose winners and losers.

This is in contrast to earlier times when money bought access and achieved power, influence, and more importantly, personal economic benefit from corrupt politicians. In America, this economic power could especially be manipulated during the years of the transcontinental railroads, steel and power brokers such as the Union Pacific Railroad and the Credit Mobilier scandal of the 1880s. Money was leveraged in concert with government leaders to achieve real economic and political power.

In response to great wars, The Great Depression, the Energy Crisis and Stagflation of the 1970s, and the dot.com boom of the 1990s the economy has continuously re-structured itself one market sector at a time. America's economic evolutions created change and became the motivation for individuals to develop new labor skills, changing work and employment conditions, as well as the pursuit of personal advancement. Since 2000 global market competition has further complicated the marketplace, it has forced changes and placed a new demand on labor, requiring advancement of new generational skillsets and individual knowledge.

Politics, Economics and Knowledge

In 2010 the United States Supreme Court was asked to answer the question posed by Citizens United v. Federal Elections Commission whether contributions made to political campaigns were an expression of political free speech? The court ruled (5–4) that, "laws preventing corporations and unions from using general treasury funds for independent electioneering communications [political advertising] violated the First Amendment's guarantee of free speech." This was a quote from a Supreme Court decision. By doing so the court declared that monetary donations are an expression of free speech and candidates running for political office could receive dollars from companies and citizens alike; it effectively removed the caps stipulated in other campaign election laws by declaring them unlawful.

In any society, any risk taken (individual, economic or political) can result in individual growth and intellectual expansion thus producing new achievements. The opposite may also happen; a loss of wealth or restricted freedom caused by new government regulations and prohibitions. In other instances individuals and organizations are sometimes accused and judged by today's media and social networks without substantive proof, but rather by simple accusation, inference or association. For example, the media and others in positions of power determined that by association the TEA (Taxed Enough Already) Party members were guilty of unacceptable retro-think rather than free political speech. In a free society it is the accusations in media and social networks that pose the greatest threats to individual freedom.

However, when citizens band together to oppose a political direction of the government, the government through its legal and regulatory processes can object, restrict or limit the activities of such groups. In America this is what happened to many local TEA Party organizations that opposed, on political terms, the laws, tax policies and regulations of the federal government. Under existing tax law, local non-profit organizations can apply for 501-C status in order to raise money. This method allows organizations of all types to accept donations on a tax deductible basis to pursue and support their intended not-for-profit purposes. The TEA Party, as a political non-profit, would raise money for political candidates opposed to recent tax increases, in particular the Affordable Healthcare Act (Obamacare). As this fundraising effort supported declared candidates opposed to the new healthcare tax, the government, through the Internal Revenue Service (IRS), initiated a time-consuming, slow walk review, to evaluate and approve their fundraising efforts in order to dissuade and reduce the money available to candidates who opposed the new law.

This review was used to delay, deny or restrict the organization's actions based upon an interpretation of intent by bureaucrats as to the organization's real intended purpose. Furthermore, by implementing a slow bureaucratic process the government effectively negated the efforts of any organization to receive contributions, further weakening the ability to raise necessary funds for the organization's expenses that could either support or oppose many political candidate issues. Rather than supporting political free speech the government was able to limit and restrict the free expression of political thought.

In America the politician's *risk* entails the potential loss of political office and not much more; if that loss were to occur prior political experience can still be leveraged into a new special interest position, especially at the federal level. Political risk in America is connected to the preservation and access to power; it is only during periods of great turmoil that a politician may experience real risk. For example, most senators are also lawyers. Their ability to leverage prior political office in concert with legal expertise makes all former senators valuable commodities in the legal and lobbying industry.

The same limited risk also applies to federal and other government employees such as bureaucrats, teachers, city planners, and managers, where virtually no employment risk exists since the system is designed to preserve the functions of government, and by doing so protects the bureaucrat. As the institutional cost of government is paid for by the tax payer without choice, the process and application of power is sustained. This low risk is shared by all the levels of government: federal, state, local, university, colleges, educational systems and most regulated monopolies.

This risk, however, does not apply to the military as soldiers not only risk life and limb in defense of the nation, but also experience employment risk as they serve based on enlistment contracts and the needs of the military. Municipal and state police and fire prevention forces are less subject to the military contract, but are exposed to violence and physical risk nonetheless, which often has an alternative outcome. These conditions set them apart from all other government employees. If teachers and other public employees were evaluated based on specific contracts or risk measured performance outcomes, would governments be viewed differently? Employment risk is not a condition of public employment.

Rare is the government that applies market considerations and measurements to employee performance; rather the employee is measured by his or her contribution to the overarching purpose of the department or agency to which they are assigned, and not to where the measurement of productivity is an essential measurement of outcome. However, dissatisfaction and discontentment, as in any job, can be present, and public employees, more than any other groups, are willing to suffer through the discontent rather than seek new employment with risk income insecurity and the related loss of positional power.

Public unions might also argue that to use market considerations to evaluate government jobs is an impossible task. To evaluate jobs requires using measurements such as efficiency, cost-management, goal measured outputs, revenue and profit determinants; these are for the most part inconsistent with the public purpose process of government and as such these measurements are inadequate. As long as government views itself differently the argument for risk does not apply, and the effective measurement of performance versus the achievement of purpose remains disproportionate when the cost of government is considered.

Risk then is not universally shared between the political, social and economic environments; risk only applies to the social and economic realms. Government's risk and that of its employees (the bureaucracy) is transferred to the public; its sole domain remains the application of power and the application of its governmental processes. Thus is created a new elite: the Political Class. This is not unlike the elites of the French pre and post-revolution—the bourgeoisie—who were later ostracized and punished, or the Soviet *Nomenklatura* and Functionaries (the political class) of the Marxist Revolution who were deemed necessary for the advancement and protection of the classless society. In either case, the idyllic *utopian* proletariat (common man) that inspired these revolutions produced unsuccessful results. The outcome is the result of many leaders who followed social re-constructionist philosophies which inspired revolutions with promises that were subscribed to and fought for by so many, and which, in the end, benefited so few.

This new political class is, in reality, answerable to no one. Yes, we have elections and yes, we have investigations, but elections are often exercised based on ideology rather than the government and the bureaucracies' performances. As a result—and through this process—government is able to control any threats to its power that may be created by legislative bodies and their partisan oversight functions, or by the bureaucracies themselves, who control and reveal only that information which is beneficial to the promotion and protection of their purposes.

This, however, does not reflect government's inability to deliver on promises made for the general betterment of the lives of its citizenry *if* its purpose is to protect basic human rights, knowledge, risk and free market conditions. These are the critical components which produce gains in the improvement of life for the common man.

In the absence of personal risk the greatest threat exists when the government reaches beyond its very purpose of "to serve" and exchanges it for "to provide." Through this mechanism the promise of public benefit is created as power is gained by the government. This is the effective exchange of political power; a promise today to deliver a future benefit, regardless of its real outcome.

Under these circumstances, government effectively supplants the idea that man assumes risk to satisfy personal needs and wants, and through this exchange, reduces motivation to the basic levels of "physiological" and "safety" needs. By reducing individual risk the citizen gives up some independence, financial resources, motivation and the desire for success, and, exchanges it for the political idea of safety, social benefit, economic security and political certainty. This is the European model of modern day socialism.

One might argue that government's efforts on behalf of health and welfare are reasonable as they target those most in need; the elderly, lower income groups and those dependent on the provision of safety net programs. These programs serve and provide assistance to those segments of our population which are the most desperate and in need of public assistance. Determining the extent of their need is difficult, so programs are created to satisfy the greatest number of people and address the greatest perceived need.

The creation of benefit, and presumption of oversight, is unlimited in its definition; the government funds national defense, education, social security, healthcare, transportation, public works, science and exploration, and it provides funding for public housing, neighborhood and central city redevelopment; it insures mortgages (FNMA, FHA), depositors (FDIC), investors (SIPC), and it regulates the environment, energy, airlines, railroads, banks and insurance companies. It is also the lender or rescuer of last resort.

The concept of public assistance for those in need appears to have long been settled and justified politically as a result of negative market conditions, the threat of disastrous economic and unemployment reports, declining or stagnant wage data, and increasing poverty levels; these all combine to produce the need for a new political and governmental solution. Given such historical reporting conditions one must ask if there has been adequate research to determine the efficacy of such programs and their outcomes, the need for regulation, length of benefits, and the need for re-education and skills training for re-employment? Do these programs effectively assist in advancing, bridging or saving people during times of great personal duress? Does the assistance move quickly enough to produce the desired results? Is there adequate funding to insure income stability? Is the market supported or hindered by regulation? Does the cost to business as a result of regulation, hamper the creation and expansion of business and new jobs? The answers depend on the issues and the arguments that can be made as well as the level of political intrigue associated with each. One can only arrive at a simple predetermined conclusion: Having created a benefit, the government will rarely, if ever, vote to reduce or eliminate it. This position is best exemplified by the passage of the Affordable Care Act and the numerous attempts to repeal it. Even though many of these programs have demonstrated to be less than successful, Congress, nor the President, would ever vote to approve the modification or termination of these social programs.

In response to these questions and the need to justify the government's supporting role there exists great volumes of statistical data attesting to the greatness and necessity of such programs. Programs designed not only to benefit members of society but also benefitting those in authority and supporting the maintenance of power. This expansion of government focuses power and ensures that government continues to grow rather than applying these resources to the original and limited purposes of government. Through such means, the actions of government changes the very fabric of the social and economic contract between the citizenry and its government. Consequently, personal risk, intellectual and monetary investment, and competition are reduced.

> *"Emergencies have always been the pretext on which the safeguards of individual liberty have been eroded.*
>
> *Even the striving for equality, by means of a directed economy, can result only in an officially enforced inequality—an authoritarian determination of the status of each individual in the new hierarchical order.*
>
> *It seems to me that socialists today can preserve their position in academic economics merely by the pretense that*

the differences are entirely moral questions about which science cannot decide."

~Friedrick August von Hayek, The Road to Serfdom

As personal risk in the economy slows, the creation of new industries and jobs are also reduced. In the end this changes the very nature of work, risk and reward. As individual risk declines the argument is made for government to sustain safety net programs based on the "emergencies" of the day and to expand on-going support. The demand for such programs expands the dialogue increasing government's power and functions. Rather than politicians examining the use of tax dollars and their social consequences, the decision is made to assuage the electorate and expand individual support. In the process government reduces, rather than improves, the nation's competitive position vis-a-vis the rest of the world. In the short term, benefits are created, yet in the long term, harm is done to the economy, creating deeper social segmentation, less intellectual capital, less risk, fewer jobs and lower middle incomes.

PART II

THE FUNDAMENTALS

ESSENTIAL # 2: THE REALITIES OF POWER AND COMPETITION; LEADERSHIP: THE CAUSAL DETERMINANT

4

GROUP DYNAMICS: THE OUTPUT DETERMINANT

THE PRODUCTION CHALLENGE

Every economic system in its own way defines individual opportunity creating within each person the desire for change and the search for opportunity. Furthermore, each of these systems is both the creator and impediment to future social and economic opportunity; each contingent on its own economic and political system, constitutional structure, adherence to the rule of law and its political leadership.

In America, the need for economic leadership began with industrialization. Prior to that time farms needed hands for plowing, weeding, and harvesting; labor was the primary determinant of the American farm not management and leadership. Industrialization changed all that, and it evolved based upon the impact and influence of money, labor, location, technology, unions, access to markets and urbanization.

Prior to the 19th and 20th centuries, the need for leadership and management was limited, economically, politically and militarily. While leadership was often viewed as self-evident, it often failed to meet the true definition of leadership as labor was readily available and replaceable at low cost, and/or expendable. Leadership's skill was dependent upon status and often blurred by the political nature of the job—its power and source emanated from a status and social class, rather than knowledge and skill.

In the 20th Century European economics changed; and social conditions allowed for the introduction of extreme forms of socialism, fascism and communism. These were the three-forms of government in which power was retained and centralized at the highest levels. Tyranny was given a formal name, and policies were implemented by leadership under the guise that change was beneficial regardless of the social cost. The economy was controlled and decisions were made which society was obligated to follow. Under these conditions the individual risked a loss of opportunity, liberty or even life. Out of fear, escape—the search for a better life —and opportunity, became the primary driving force within the existing social system.

Capitalist societies offered different challenges in contrast to socialism, fascism and communism.

In America, in early business models, profit was the primary objective. Business models utilized high numbers of low cost labor to achieve productivity. During the early industrialization periods of the 19th century such models worked, and profit was achieved at the expense of labor. Later, unions formed and came into power; often the union controlled the hiring, not so much the number, but the "who" of who was to be employed. Hiring decisions were made based upon social and familial connections, heritage, race, etc. During this period of time leadership was limited to its singular objective: earn a profit. This was a simple and mechanical process so long as the product being produced had readily available markets allowing revenue to be generated and profits earned.

As economic progress occurred social needs evolved, as did America's social complexity. The result of these ameliorating factors was immigration, culture, language, education, work opportunities, income, and, in today's latest technological evolution, the social/business network. All became part of the redefinition of the work environment and the pursuit of success. In this new model the economy was no longer dependent upon the political position or class position of the owners; but rather the creativity of the individual.

Capitalism is driven by knowledge, experience, creativity, risk, competition, innovation, opportunity and profit, and motivated self-interest rather than the consolidation of power or position. Profit is subject to the efficiency of the production system, its creativity and innovation. It is driven by effective leadership and management in which operational challenges are considered, and effective solutions applied. Combined these produce the technological surprise of new products.

Today, earning a profit isn't as easy. In each step the existence of knowledge, personalities, corporate values, market competition, product development/design, work rules, safety standards, sourcing of materials, training and re-training, technology, production, accounting, finance, capital investment, regulation, taxes and so forth, must all be considered. Meanwhile the desired outcome hasn't changed; profit remains the end state. However, the essentials of the earlier industrialization period, and the basic idea of products driven by price, consumption and competitive markets, remain. Profit remains the primary driver for any business, for without it business cannot compete nor sustain itself.

Every organization then is confronted with the need to achieve the purposes for which it was created. Every business must work to affirm its purpose daily within the competitive marketplace, and every organization must reexamine each aspect of its business model, continuously measuring progress against pre-established principles and goals that describe the organization's intent and purpose. Each business is challenged by the very nature of its organization: its capacity to achieve and its values as specified by management, employees, responsibilities, personalities and products. Internally, every group evolves to address their function and each individual is measured against the group's contribution to the whole.

By measuring each individual's performance against the organization's goals and objectives, it asks the question: How does a leader manage, through the complexity of the organization, its product, production, personalities and internal politics, to achieve its greatest potential? Through this process the challenge of leadership and individual responsibility is developed. In the end the totality of the organization's effort is measured simply by either its success or failure.

An effective knowledgeable leader must be able to recognize the forces at play as quickly as possible since the dynamic can reduce the overall effectiveness of any effort in the short term, lengthen the time to completion, or eliminate any possibility of accomplishing the task. The leader that succumbs to the resistance of the group eliminates the possibility of achieving the desired outcome. To overcome this, the leader must have a clear vision of the objective and the goal, effectively communicate it, and lead from the onset.

Within the group, and conditioned upon the nature of the

group, leadership and managerial action is often required to achieve progress. Under certain conditions this can be difficult to achieve as progress is affected by the private or public nature of the organization, and the presence of organized or dysfunctional management and labor. The ability of the leader to recognize this dynamic is essential. Depending on leadership action or inaction, the success of the organization can either be enhanced or diminished; if the later, failure can occur quickly. Alternatively, an organization with new but weak leadership will remain stagnant over time, in which case the internal and cumulative resistance to change will delay/postpone any chance of success, again ending in failure.

Effective leadership, by intent, is the primary driver of the dynamic, pushing the organization to institute new directions which can be, but need not be, radical in its redirection. Leadership should establish the direction, define the overarching principles, set goals and measure progress towards their achievement, instituting new methodologies that re-think processes and redefine outcomes. Leadership should be knowledgeable about the organization, its structure and its products; however, in times of need, leadership should not be afraid to recruit from the outside to change the fundamentals of institutional think. The objective of leadership should be to create a structural agility able to withstand internal pressures and market competition.

Equally important for any organization or society, is to select, review, and promote future leaders. Within any organization, as within society, it is important for individuals to recognize and evaluate their leaders based on past social, economic and political success as determined by their objective outcomes; which in turn impacts the private or public, local or national, advancement.

. . .

Leadership Types

Over the years I have had the privilege to see and study different leaders. Each was distinct, and their effectiveness in addressing problems reflected in how each approached and solved problems. When considering managers and leaders it should be noted there is a great difference between a supervisor, a manager and a leader: supervisors are task responsible; managers are focused on goals and objectives as defined by senior management; and leaders determine the vision, the goals and objectives, the essential future think which guides the organization and which will be used to determine future investment and market position. Skill sets are extraordinarily different in time and function at each level, commensurate with their organizational responsibility.

The following is a brief reflection of different leadership styles and their approaches to management. For ease of use--and memory--I have labeled them : (1) By the Numbers, (2) The Biggest Loser, (3) The Protector, (4) The Idea Man, (5) The Producer, (6) The General, (7) Starters, (8) The Imagined and (9) Excellence Pursued. Identifying them has allowed me to differentiate one type from another, and to distinguish them easily.

By the Numbers

"Check the Box"

The By the Numbers leader is a box checker. He is often a long-term employee of the company and obtained his leadership position by virtue of familiarity with corporate and production processes. The measurement of production and statistical outcomes are his forte, he has seniority in both the organization and knows its product and production. When speaking to a box checker you discover that there is great familiarity with his job/task; the job is handled in a perfunctory manner, driven by procedure and accuracy of outcome, all performed by the numbers.

Checkers are methodical, although they may have limited interpersonal management skills, instead relying on the power of position and seniority and demanding performance of others. They may use their position of power to comment on a workers performance to motivate including informal opportunities to inform employees and others of personal successes and failures of execution.

Checkers are "sequencers" whose primary intent is to check the box; their performance is statistical, measured month to month or quarter to quarter. No employee error or achievement is too big or too small to mention in order to preserve the power of the Checker.

This management style can create a stifling work environment with a sense of constant oversight which overpowers staff; a supervisory style which management will need to address to improve morale and productivity. This may include training to improve management and communication skills with the hope that effective leadership can produce a better work environment and increase productivity.

If positioned at a senior level this management style reduces the motivation of employees seeking the path to success, they in turn will, in time, quit or ask for transfers.

The Biggest Loser

"Number One"

The Loser's management style should be avoided. Incompetence is their hallmark masked by good speech, but with no vision or effective strategy to achieve the objective. Losers use their business and political acumen to gain management positions to advance their careers, but they are most likely to become destructive of the organization and its purpose. They seek, and obtain, jobs in far-apart locations where their reputations are least likely to be known or deeply examined. They use the basic rule of "you look out for number one" to justify all management decisions and actions. As "number one" everyone else, including the organization, may be expendable. If the Loser is protected by contract, in the short term he will survive at the expense of the organization, but in the long term great damage will be done.

These leaders are effective communicators externally but never clearly state internal strategies and objectives, rather letting team members define their personal and organizational goals, even if internal conflict is created. By shifting responsibility they shift the blame for failures to others avoiding any personal responsibility. These managers further limit their accessibility by limiting access. They also avoid questions and decisions which address critical issues. As absent leaders they use corporate resources to their benefit, and to the detriment of the organization and its management team.

Losers accuse and blame other associates for failed outcomes. When necessary, and if outcomes don't match their vision in the moment, they--often in concert with other employees--will make known other team member failures and will use this to justify termination. Losers protect their position and move to eliminate possible threats to their power regardless of the source. Under this management style many professional staff resign their position resulting in a weakened company with the possibility of a future business collapse.

As the head of the organization, and using these techniques, Losers never need to justify decisions or absences, placing blame for failure to achieve objectives on others within the organization.

Losers are the worst kind of leader using smoke screens to hide their own failures. Losers are narcissistic with the primary intent of self-promotion; they measure their own success by the adulation they receive from outside sources. Enron's senior management fit into this category, as do many historical and modern day political leaders.

The Protector

"I'll fix it."

The "Protector" is the leader who works to make sure that he has the right team in place and is leading in the right direction. However, as a leader he is willing to overlook team member weaknesses and failures in the short term with the idea that over time all problems can be overcome and success achieved. The Protector is less the leader and more the manager. He listens, encourages, and approaches failures as problems of execution, not as failures of team members. He is the greatest of friends and supporter of the individual. He is a defender of the weak, and of the status quo.

Personally he struggles the most during times of change, the realities of the market, and the much needed and required change in business direction. For the Protector it is far better to fine tune business practices rather than face the major challenges directly. He will avoid the need for change in hopes that current market conditions will revert to prior circumstances. The Protector is a "pleaser" whose primary intent is to manage the business in its present form, focus on fine tuning the organization, and ensuring the commitment of employees to it.

He measures his own success through the preservation of the organization and evolution of the business supporting all employees in the process. He gives from the heart; he is a caring and principled leader. The Protector will argue against change to prevent organizational disruption, and through his leadership, protect even the least performing.

The Idea Man

"Imagine This"

The Idea Man is the most dynamic of all management types driven by the single idea that drives his leadership style: personal recognition. The Idea Man is the most affable and demonstrative leader pushing new ideas, baking them with emotional appeal and seeking reward through both monetary means and corporate recognition. He speaks of potential successes and their ability to affect great outcomes. Idea Men have the greatest imagination, pushing for the greatest outcomes, but in their passion they struggle to delineate the means and the quantifiable benefits to the organization. Idea Men rely heavily on their energy and ability to sway listeners, and convince them of the correctness of their ideas. With the right audience this approach has enormous impact on the organization imbuing it with similar zeal.

The Idea Man surrounds himself with like-minded dreamers

that struggle to translate their verbiage into quantifiable results. The Idea Man is in need of partners/team members that can translate dreams into measurable products, benefits and outcomes. His primary intent is to utilize new technologies to create change, and products using self-promotion and energy as the means to accomplish the change. Idea Men need an audience so they are among the most vocal and endearing manager types.

The Producer

"More, Produce More"

The Producer is a demanding and vocal leader, he is driven by performance, his own as well as those that work with him and for him. Failure by employees to achieve the demanded higher performance standard results in rebuke, and perhaps, a demotion, or the ultimate reassignment - dismissal. The Producer demands performance by laying out goals for all employees, goals which may be achieved only by individuals seeking the greatest possible reward and gain for themselves. For a Producer every day, every week, every month and every year must have the highest level of performance. To measure success, every time period has its own performance standard, each created and measured against past performance, with goals established for the next. For the Producer the established standard of performance cannot be stated enough; results are the only accurate measurement of corporate success. Producer companies tend to be focused on core products with sales and benefits defined by the product itself: real estate, energy and finance companies for example. Companies led by Producers tend to have the most competitive employees and the highest turnover rates in entry level positions.

Starters

"Risk, it's the name of the game!"
Entrepreneurs are the sustenance of every economy and are the leading force in the free market; they establish businesses based on their ability to find success through the delivery of goods to the market place. Starters are willing risk takers investing their own money, and perhaps that of others, in the hope that they will achieve better results through satisfying market needs, creating new ideas, and growing their own personal wealth. They see openings in the market place and rush to fill it. To do this, Starters are often driven by their own vision of the market, and are totally focused upon the outcomes, such as: cash flows, product, competition and the challenge of profitability. If new to the business, prior management experience may be limited; however, if the Starter does have industry knowledge and experience, he is driven by production and the goal of being successful in his own right and against his competition with unique products.

Entrepreneurs can be effective leaders in small organizations directing employees to accomplish differentiated tasks; stretching and testing every employee's skills set to their limits. In the process they provide education and skills development for their employees in a deep and concentrated fashion. Starters are challenging leaders, creating expectations that may or may not be achievable. Given the vagaries of the businesses, Starters may seek short cuts which, in the end, may come at a great expense to the business. In this instance, leadership may be short-sighted and the outcome may be negative. Consequently, in competitive markets, small businesses have high failure rates. A Starter's leadership is a reflection of his ability to manage and lead, creating success for himself and his business in the market place while building staying power in the long term.

> *"Entrepreneurs provide a continuing challenge both to men who refuse a practical engagement in the world, on the grounds that it is too dangerous or corrupt, and to men who demand power over others in the name of ideology or expertise without first giving and risking themselves and their wealth.*
>
> *Capitalism offers nothing but frustrations and rebuffs to those who, by virtue of their superior intelligence, birth, credentials, or ideals, believe themselves entitled to get without giving, to take without risking, to profit without understanding, and to be exalted without humbling themselves to meet the unruly demands of others in an always perilous and unpredictable life."*
>
> *-George Gilder, Knowledge and Power, page 277*

The General

"Strategic in thought and practice"

The General is the silent leader; he fully understands the business and the means to achieve success. He has a clear vision of the business, the market, and the organization. He defines the organization's business model and targets customers establishing direct and insightful leadership. There is no question, in or outside the organization, as to its direction and uniqueness in the marketplace. He further surrounds himself with the best people, not for political reasons but for structure and effectiveness. He modifies the model as necessary to help it achieve even greater success in the market place of ideas, products and profit. The model is modified, not reactively, but rather in a thoughtful way to recognize the organizations strengths, market position and potential.

The General never puts the company at risk, but executes adjustments to market conditions in an effective methodical planned way, providing for constancy of corporate outcome. The General is the unchallenged leader whose primary intent is the success of the organization; he measures his own success in parallel with the identity and success of the institution he leads. Leaders of this type may best be exemplified by military leaders that see the battlefield in its entirety, strategic in thought and action, measuring all possibilities and choosing the appropriate course of action resulting in success at achieving the stated objective. The General's management style is rooted in deep personal experience and learned principles.

Imagined

"What if?"

Imagined leaders represent the innovator, the person who creates change by fundamentally redefining behavior in the context of innovation and markets. *Imaginators* imagine and ask "what if" or "is this possible?" Today the world is experiencing the greatest era of creative and scientific-technical evolutionary advancement. *Imaginators* leverage fundamental technical knowledge into ideas and products which maybe physical, intellectual and/or emotional. They require a combination of hardware and software to operate. Regardless of the product, somewhere in the system these products run in the forefront or the background of every technology. *Imaginators* create products that expand human action and interaction, and feed the never-ending desire for personal satisfaction.

With the right idea, the world--not just America--becomes the market. And, along with the new expanded world markets, extraordinary profits and wealth are created in a very short period of time. The larger the consumer market, the greater the possibility of revenue, and creation of personal and corporate wealth.

In this marketplace the leadership of the *Imaginator* is challenged since he is more interested in the promotion and advancement of the product. *Imaginators* rely upon hired expertise to manage the company's expanding employment, technological resources and benefits that feed the never-ending need for speed, creativity and capital. The more innovative the original idea, and the larger the market, the greater the demand for skilled employment producing great reward for the services performed. For the innovator the pressure to create and produce is the upper-most goal; for the employee the opportunity to create, and the challenge of the product, results in great reward and satisfaction. The exchange is one of pay-for-knowledge; the need is to constantly evolve the product to ever higher levels of consumer benefit and satisfaction.

> *"Information is the unexpected "surprise" that when incorporated into the system creates growth and surplus value— wealth". Rev. Johannes Jacobs, Acton, on George Gilder, Knowledge and Power.*

Excellence Pursued

"Excellence isn't an aspiration, it's a personal standard.
Let me take you there!"

The leader focused on Excellence is the best leader; he dignifies every employee, customer, and any other person he comes in contact with. The Excellence-focused leader understands the workings of the business top to bottom, and is easily the best at executing the business plan from a management and leadership perspective. He has the clearest of visions for the company he leads. He demonstrates his leadership by placing himself in a subservient way to his fellow employees by asking simple questions such as: "What can I do to make each and every employee successful?" "Is there anything I can do personally for each of you?" Each employee has been validated, each willing to perform at the highest level, and each expressing confidence in management and leadership. As market changes affect the business, this leader seeks to ensure continuing employee success through innovation, evolving the vision and goals of the company to meet market conditions. By expressing concern for each individual, and knowing that mission-success relies solely upon the creativity of each individual as applied to the focus of the business, individual success ultimately contributes to total organizational success.

Excellence is achieved through innovation, vision, management of cost, and the development of effective strategies that produce corporate and individual success. This leader is also a realist knowing the limitations of the business and what must be changed to ensure long term success. He is the leader of the business, the primary motivator and the servant of those in his employ. He recognizes that the business is the means to accomplish the vision and the objective. He is known for the man he is, and measures his own success through the profits earned and the achievement of those he leads.

> *"Treat your men as you would your own beloved sons. And they will follow you into the deepest valley."*
> *~Sun Tzu, The Art of War*

Effective leadership acknowledges operational and market conditions while building the necessary processes that reach beyond the obvious; leadership that designs new concepts and products for future success. Effective leadership acknowledges each aspect of the business/organization and measures each component that contributes to the whole; leadership that must set goals, implement and advance production, and adjust accordingly.

> *"Strategy without tactics is the slowest route to victory. Tactics without strategy is the noise before defeat."*
> *~Sun Tzu, The Art of War*

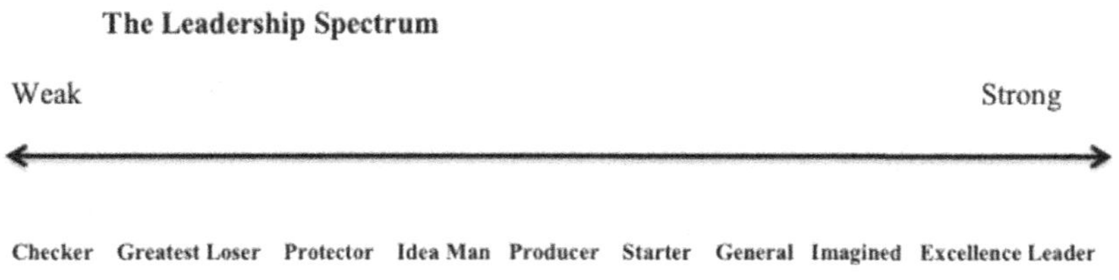

One such leader, recognized and admired by many, is Jack Welch, former CEO of General Electric (GE). When he became the head of GE he was challenged by the age and culture of the company, its products and direction. He decided that the company needed to evolve to become a company of the future. However, unlike most managers, he approached this problem differently. He determined that if the company was to succeed he would have to change the very culture of the company; one which he perceived as stagnant. Innovation had taken a back seat to the status quo with a culture dominated by routine and established thinking. Employees believed they had a right to their jobs, and accepted the idea of their permanence. Unions had effectively negotiated for benefits, work conditions, regular and over-time pay, and had long since accepted the idea that market levels wouldn't affect or change their jobs. The expectation was that products and market conditions would remain relatively constant as would their jobs. However, with the advent of global competition, all pre-existing ideas regarding products and technology would change. GE would have to compete effectively in new markets against more efficient producers. For Welch the leadership question was, given GE's present organization model and products could it compete?

The challenge for him was how to address the moribund nature of GE. He decided that there needed to be a re-establishment of the competitive mindset within the corporate structure; a new employment model would be needed to achieve this in a globally competitive marketplace; he would have to change the employment paradigm. His solution: All employees would have to compete to retain their jobs, not just in the labor force; but management as well. No longer would life-time employment be assured; the success of the company would come first. To do this he issued an order stating that the company would reduce their labor force by 10 percent with each department evaluating their employees and the lowest performing employee(s) furloughed regardless of position. GE would support this transition by offering programs and packages to assist employees in seeking new employment. What Welch created was a change in the company's dynamic/group think. Pressure was applied to the *employee think* with the realization that jobs were dependent upon individual knowledge, performance and a competitive employment market.

Jack Welch recognized that within every organization there needs to be a desire to succeed, and this success has to be readily visible within the organization if it is to complete its mission. Regardless of the organization's private or public nature the same conditions would exist.

Every organization must continuously evaluate itself, its products and its processes which are all designed to motivate and accomplish its purpose; to remain focused on its vision, and the necessary means to achieve it. The process of evaluating every employee's contribution to the whole is essential. Some companies/organizations measure this contribution based on the number of tasks completed and the contribution to the whole, while others use broad-based job specific objectives. Others, still, use quantifiable outputs, or contributions to the whole versus profit.

Along with determining the measurement tool, the process of leadership is further complicated by clearly delineating the organization, its purpose and its primary motivating factor, profit or other standards. In evaluating employees, organizations must establish clear measurable standards that stand the test of time, as well as today's court challenges. To do so companies use strict objectives and performance measurements. However defined, for leadership it remains necessary to tune the organization for productive results, an objective that may be difficult to ascertain and achieve given the size of the organization.

The challenge for any effective leader is to consider the makeup of the organization and to delineate its structure. In the process it is necessary to identify the functions that are most important to its success, and to measure each function and its contribution to the whole. This is critical since the dynamic of the organization is directly dependent upon the strength of its intellectual capital and the extent of its resources. To understand this dynamic it is necessary to understand the organizational structure and department and employee interactions.

The first step in the process is to identify and select the leaders/managers that help the organization achieve its pursuits, for without them none of the organization's objectives can be achieved. Leaders must be chosen that advance the organization's vision and objectives. Failing to do so leads to less productive outcomes and less profitable results, however measured. Leaders must not only have a vision for the company, but lead by *applying moral principles, recognizing legal constraints, and practicing ethical behavior in relationships* with employees and customers. These three concepts, moral, legal and ethical, must be united in the leader to achieve effective outcomes and advance the purposes of the organization.

All companies use some form of production measurement, however, to be effective these processes must be accompanied by equally effective human management. Charles Koch of Koch Industries created a different strategy for their employees developing principles that are more focused on core behaviors similar to the rights a nation might guarantee its citizens. Using such principles as integrity, entrepreneurship and knowledge the company has advanced employees, created new products and entered markets around the world.

Every leader must understand his/her team, defining its limitations, capabilities and interactions. Doing so establishes the means of achieving and determining the organizations future success; therefore, the role organizational subgroup's play must also be considered as part of this evaluative process to determine the overall effectiveness of the organization.

As a leader it is essential to recognize that the more complex the work force the more likely there are to be sub-groups, the manager's challenge is to develop a management strategy for each production group which is defined by the demands of the organization, as well as the production needs of the group. The interpersonal relations/conditions that exist within these sub-groups further define the success or the failure of the organization.

Essential to every organization are its workers, without which there is no product or progress. Their active involvement in achieving the goals of the organization is critical to its success. Over time, and throughout my career, I have identified three personality/subgroup characteristics which directly impact the progress of all organizations: Vocals, Rollovers and Outsiders. Their brief descriptions are shown here:

Vocals...

1. Are self-satisfied
2. Express themselves the loudest in any meeting or gathering, and attempt to dominate any conversation
3. Speak of the need for change
4. But, will defend the status quo and oppose change
5. New ideas and change are hardest to accept

6. Have a need to know the details and will use the details to object to the change
7. Will consider the situation, but will find reasons / justifications to object to the change in circumstance and condition
8. Will see opportunity as a problem, opportunity causes change, and with change their self-perceived position of recognition and power is impacted
9. Individuals will/push seek power when supported by the group
10. They are the final act of resistance, and will be the last to adopt new directions; once change is implemented they will continue to oppose the new direction

Rollovers...

1. These are the undecided members of the group
2. Watch and listen to the dynamic, but opt to not act
3. Are the last to commit
4. Will bend to the wishes of the group without taking a position
5. May or may not be part of the inner circle
6. Are followers or subscribers to the group think
7. Have a need to know but not decide
8. Are risk averse and practice conflict avoidance
9. Will wait for the change then buy in and support after the fact
10. May see a problem but will wait for someone else to act
11. Are willing to accept change as a part of the job
12. Are willing to accept the outcome without objection

13. Are willing to work towards achieving the goals of the group

Outsiders...

1. Self-aware
2. May or may not be a first adopter, questions new ideas
3. Change must have purpose, be deliberate, and not be just rhetoric
4. Knows the job, understands the details, knows the practice and is willing to move beyond the present circumstance
5. Independent critical thinker, doer, takes ownership of the task
6. Recognizes opportunity and/or the problem
7. Contributes to the development of productive ideas and objectives, avoids non-productive conversation
8. Risk taker
9. Measures involvement and applies appropriate response
10. Personal achievement and success flow from being a part of the solution and the change process.
11. May, in the end, be the most isolated and thus most unwilling to contribute to the process of change given the group dynamic
12. Source of future management
13. May be the first to leave the organization in pursuit of greater success and new opportunity.

Cautions:

Leadership without a clear understanding of an organization's future and the problems it faces is often unable to clearly state or define the objectives of the organization. Organizations focused on short term objectives, with no clear long term plan and strategy, will result in starts and stops as the organization struggles and searches for an effective success strategy to achieve its primary purpose. The clearer the organization's statement of purpose and objectives, the easier it is to define the path to success.

The Vocal as a leader:

Vocals are great talkers and have a great passion to be heard and they will always support the organization's need to evolve. But, when a vocal is chosen to be a leader, a complication is introduced; other vocals will support the leader, but will resist the new agenda. As a friend, the vocal leader will listen to and promote the vocal group's agenda which, contrary to leaderships intent, remains the preservation of the status quo. The opportunity for change is then redefined and limited as the vocal leader will side with the others to resist or oppose change unless exchanged for additional benefit.

The vocal leader will tackle easy challenges and claim victory--the check the box standard but will avoid difficult challenges or significant change as it goes against the Vocals' ethos. In the end, when promoted to such a position, the Vocal leader will unknowingly practice *symbolic modernization*; talk about the change, promote the need for change, but *never* implement the change. The Vocal leader requires the support of other vocals in order to gain and sustain power. And, as he is emotionally connected to the group, supporting the greater organization's agenda is a risk that he may not be willing to, or is unprepared to take. Any vision that the vocal may have is limited by the very nature of friendship and will defer to the power of the group rather than the need of the organization. At this point he is unable to clearly state or execute the corporate vision, purpose and direction.

The Sideliner: The Sideliner is the inside-the-organization observer who stands on the sideline, watching, expressing thought and opinion, reporting, but having no real knowledge to form a valid opinion. The Sideliner lacks experience within the group, often just a friend, adding input where none is sought, but offering compassionate support; a member whose voice, knowledge and experience are topic-limited. His views, while discounted by management, are acknowledged by members of the Vocal and Rollover groups as valid concerns, providing the opposition with support on issues and positions. They are the voiced expression of resistance and opposition to change. The Sideliner is a friend of the group, connected by employment and social interaction, and may or may not be measured by the same objective performance measurements. He is often among those that speak the loudest to cover their lack of real knowledge and experience. He is the sports fan that is knowledgeable about the game and can opine on every play, but rarely plays.

The Saboteur: The saboteur often works alone--only occasionally with others--to kill the possibility of the success of others. The saboteur is unwilling to accept their current position as it may be perceived as being beneath their talent and skills. This person works silently against outsiders to affect the overall outcomes; they spread rumors against individuals; pointing out a rival's perceived weaknesses, and taking every opportunity to enhance their own credibility, including exchanging information for the benefit of management's recognition. Effective leaders recognize and discount the saboteur. Weak managers (checkers and losers) will use the saboteur to develop information on other employees to gain position or build a case against them, which can then be acted upon by management. It is the worst of leadership tactics to use gossip and lies to reduce the standing of fellow employees.

Considering the wide variety of personalities and characters, it is easy to understand the complexity of organizational dynamics. The number of potential leaders and subgroups can create 27 possible permutations representing all levels of status from the most senior level manager down to the production worker, each supported by different employee sub-groups. However, the number itself excludes the mid-level manager(s), and when combined with this third group, the permutations become vastly even greater, and the challenge for success even more complicated and difficult.

Recognizing the above, my experience has shown that the most stimulating companies to work for are small companies in which the success of the company is fully dependent upon the entire team working together to achieve the common objectives. Well led, these small companies become corporate leaders.

The next best are midsize companies with approximately 2,000± employees. This category represents well-established companies with great products and market value, and in which they have identified marketplace niches. In this range employees are known to senior management and the leadership pool is deep. If properly led these are strong companies with the ability to create innovative products that generate robust profits and have a recognized market position and good leadership. They employ contributing and productive employees, and have well-established wage, benefit and support programs.

5

SOCIETIES, ECONOMICS AND POLITICAL POWER

EVOLUTION CHANGES EVERYTHING

Societies have risen, prospered and failed over time, their longevity and progress determined by a few cultural evolutionary factors. First, did they consume all their natural resources and in the process destroy their natural habitat? If so, did they succumb to the idea that the only remaining option was to move beyond their current location or die? Second, did society move beyond the tribal structure; did the tribe evolve to a higher social order as a result of discovery? Third, is the tribe or society capable of evolving into an independent state in which the culture and political order are not pre-determined? Was opportunity created as a result of advanced, commonly held individual knowledge and beliefs? Fourth, did this knowledge-based culture develop a political system that could provide sufficient freedom to permit the development of society into a modern nation? Fifth, did the knowledge based economic system innovate and allow for the advancement of the individual, and by extension, society? Sixth, did the political system support the advancement of the individual or did it, through the passage of laws and regulations, limit individual risk and advancement? To answer these questions one must consider the character of the culture, the development of markets, and the political structures in place.

Depending on its culture and social structure and stage of development, a society will either become stagnant--retaining its present level of social and political structure--or advance in which all aspects of society evolve to a higher social, economic and political order. Given a nation's stage of development, and its level of social knowledge and political advancement, outcomes are predictable: the state will either limit or advance the person based upon the nation's ability and willingness to modify itself.

A nation's history is a reflection of how its people develop over time, and how their national institutions evolve. History is reflected in a nation's social evolution, the lives and culture of its people, its social structures, its political struggles, and its economic advancement; progress measured by a societies ability and willingness to adjust to new conditions and circumstances. Through this evolutionary change social advancement occurs, populations grow, education levels improve, natural resources exploited, economies developed, and political philosophy and government defined. These conditions are manifest and reflected in the social, economic and political conditions that affect every individual, and every nation.

Progress then, for each nation, is measured by its ability to adjust to new circumstances, to leverage global technological change and to modernize their political structure to *compete* ideologically and economically against their neighbors, and the world at large. If a nation is unable to compete or adjust to the new condition then progress ceases and the nation drifts, neither advancing nor declining, as in the modern European experience. The nation, being controlled by the system in place, fails to advance and will only advance when a political transformation occurs replacing the existing order; until such time the nation and its people are trapped in the status quo with little or no opportunity. Such is the case with many nations around the world which remain mired in political systems that failed to evolve, countries such as North Korea, Russia, Greece, and nations in the Middle East, Africa and Central America.

To be a modern nation there are certain essentials common to all people, these include such things as a free society, entrepreneurship, and political freedom. These are mutually *interdependent* interacting and providing for the basics of social and political advancement. Without these combined essentials, nations remain under-developed retaining a tribal social structure or a central government driven by tradition; a system of centralized political control which resists and restricts the nation's ability to evolve. How a nation deals with this set of conditions will determine their ability to reject, adjust or accept evolutionary change. It determines how nations will compete with their surrounding neighbors and their ideological and economic circumstances.

The political ideology of a nation further defines the system of government (republic, socialism, totalitarianism, or theocracy) and determines the impact on its citizens. Are citizens free to act in an independent manner or, does the government or social hierarchy control them? Which has more power? Ultimately, the political system determines how the government will interact with its citizens; individual freedoms being fully dependent upon the actions of those with power and in command, whether a dictatorship or democracy. The power of government and its motivations always have outcomes that either expand the authority of government or impact the actions and freedom of its citizens. The answer to these questions will determine the ability of the individual to pursue knowledge and economic opportunity.

Individuals (dictators) may take power over a short period of time designing a political system and government that grants those in authority absolute power. This employs an ideology which convinces the average citizen that *this* government is essential to achieving the betterment of their society and culture, and that its actions are righteous. And the government is the only one suited to guide the nation in achieving its social-political reformation and economic advancement. In the process the government redefines its relationship with its citizens, and the world, using imagined or real threats against it as political weapons to sustain and control power.

In studying the evolution of modern societies the social, political and economic environments are often considered in the totality of their condition, or in the singularity of events that define them. Ultimately, in freedom limiting societies, social and political evolution or revolution will occur. Regardless of the cause, change will come and social advancement, or conflict, will follow with the social outcomes analyzed and conclusions reached based on historical personalities and events.

Is there a set form of government?

Throughout the world there are nations that declare themselves to be "free" but are more defined by the limits placed on their citizens to speak openly and freely; this is typical of systems in which power is concentrated in a single party; for example,

Russia, China and Iran. The party demands political adherence and through its practices demonstrates the unrestrained limits of its power. In doing so the party itself defines the limits of a citizen's opportunity, and by its laws, rules and application of power, justify their own political existence, and constrain the human development of their own citizens.

Republics, which are often defined as democracies, operate under the authority of popular sovereignty, a government led by the representatives of its people, and carrying out the mandates of their constituents. In this system the people grant those in power the responsibility to pursue the development of the "common good," a power which can be easily abused unless overseen and limited by the very citizens that they were elected to serve. In a republic politicians are elected to serve the needs of the people at multiple levels and may work hard to address the very problems which they were elected to solve. In doing so they pass laws which create programs, expanding bureaucracies for the benefit and advancement of the community, and through this process also expand the reach and power of government. Operating under the belief that without such laws and programs society would not be adequately served, nor would the community achieve its greatest potential. If the benefits provide a desired and effective outcome, satisfaction or social benefit, then society is well served and improved.

Throughout this process the citizen may agree to the laws and programs, but may also in the process give up some personal risk and, perhaps, freedoms in the belief that these political actions are for their benefit. In a free society this may be the greatest threat as this power is not taken surreptitiously in a single change of direction and governance, but in a slow evolutionary manner. Such power, unless overseen by responsible citizens, can, over time, be manipulated and utilized for the benefit of those in power, including the bureaucracy.

Political ideologies and governmental structures impact and define individual action, expanding or inhibiting personal motivation. Depending on circumstances the political system supports or detracts from the development of the individual; it impacts their worldview; extends or impedes the development of their society; and, affects their concept of independence.

6

BALANCING THE TENSIONS

In any Republic the social, economic and political systems are under constant stress and yet are fully interdependent, each in tension with the other two, each dependent upon the knowledge present in its citizens, its businesses, and its institutions. Through their knowledge, motivation and risk, they impact the nation as a whole. In the process, the structure itself creates motivation and the pursuit of power that advances change and produces progress in the social and economic realms.

Institutions, whether public or private, may have great power depending on the depth of their authority and money. But, by virtue of their interdependent nature and the complexity of their individual constructs, problems cannot be easily solved without affecting the broader conditions of all three. To solve social and economic problems, real and perceived, government, acting as the voice of the people, has become the preferred method to solve contentious problems. Through this political action the passage of laws and challenges in courts are undertaken. Today the courts have become the preferred means to address and solve tough social issues at the national level rather than the historical process of dialogue and the search for common ground.

If a positive outcome is created then society evolves and the economy expands and opportunity expands. If a legal or government solution is imposed then the economy is directly impacted; individuals and businesses will ultimately benefit, or pay the price, for the politically mandated solution. If a negative impact is created the health and vitality of the marketplace is directly impacted, business will comply but at cost to the quantity and quality of jobs. It is very difficult to find the optimum solution.

Under the right circumstances one individual can create awareness and challenge prevailing social conditions and markets. One individual creating technological innovation can change the economy. One individual through personal charisma and leadership may be able to reset the direction of government but not without push back from competing interests. The power of one individual can influence other citizens, and when and if they are joined and in concert, they may become powerful enough to overcome obstacles at the local, state and national levels. Such a leader acting alone cannot reset competing social and economic conditions, but through their leadership they can have enormous impacts. This, however, does not alter the desire to modify present circumstances that constrain progress. Consequently, a leader seeking to impact any of these three environments will experience an arduous process mirrored in the politics of the day in both private and public venues.

The desire *to do* politically results in new directions and new programs paid for through higher prices, taxes or fees. As a result, new programs are created expanding the bureaucracy. These government programs, however, are not evaluated based on impact or success but rather the support of politicians and special interest. And, subject to the political objectives, programs may come at the expense of individuals through either increased taxation or possible decreases in civil liberties and freedoms.

Following this model and based on this principle governments have always promised a better life delivering programs which address the fears and needs of the people, in the process gain power for themselves, seek votes and promise change--the ultimate exchange. However, the success or failure of any political system, in the near or long term, depends on a government's ability to adjust to circumstance in response to the needs of the people; prosperity or sustaining the status quo will depend on the use and application of this power.

Describing Power

Power is often described in terms of political influence, military might, economic dynamism, or group identity and alignment, but rarely is it described in terms of its fundamental characteristics. All real power leverages one or more of the following five characteristics producing different levels of control and different outcomes. It must be noted that only individuals possess all five of these traits; companies and governments leverage one, two, or three to achieve their objectives in the marketplace and political landscape. Power is executed by individuals, politicians and entrepreneurs to achieve their desired goals; but to do so requires the application of, or some combination of, the following characteristics:

(1) Information/data: (a) Individuals subject to their needs leverage information/data for personal or corporate advantage and gain. (b) Propaganda: the active promotion of information by the use of media to advance a greater corporate purpose. (c) The use of media and other communication outlets to communicate a political agenda; the partnering of the media with the government for its own benefit and power.

(2) Control: An individual's ability to manage circumstance and outcomes; the extent of government command over the governed.

(3) Righteousness: (a) The advancement of ideas which declare the actions of individuals or government to be the means to resolve problems. (b) The effectiveness in communicating the correctness of an idea; (c) a self-proclaimed moral truth; (d) acting in accord with divine or moral law.

(4) Knowledge: (a) the ability to evaluate and find solutions to questions through individual acts of discovery, education and experience; (b) the application of knowledge to the analysis of information to determine its accuracy and veracity.

(5) Risk: the willingness of an individual to act to defend or advance one's own interest, regardless of cost. Courage.

Real power is always based on these five concepts; without these elements, or combination thereof, effective power cannot be executed.

Only an individual can deploy all five characteristics to address and solve problems. However, if government becomes the means to execute solutions, then the political objective of power is achieved by employing three of these five characteristics: (1) Information, (2) Control, and (3) Righteousness—consider Germany's Hitler, Russia's Lenin and Stalin and China's Mao Tse Tung; all used these three to justify their reasons for the need for change. However these leaders ultimately devolved to just control to maintain their power, sustained by fear. Or compare President Obama and President Trump: which President had the media on their side and effectively communicated the righteousness of his position? These three concepts were leveraged to advance political solutions to common problems while simultaneously creating power for those in position to command.

Media's gain is in its establishment as an ally of political thought, direction and power with the ability to influence the righteousness and stated objection to the social issues of the day. This success is rewarded through the subsequent development and expanded power gained by both the politician as well as members of the media. The outcome is the promotion and acceptance of attitudes and political thought which advance an agenda supported by individuals, interest groups and/or government. A position antithetical to the ideas of a free non-aligned press.

The Impact of Progress

Thaddeus McCotter, former US Representative, Michigan, proposed the idea of "order, justice and freedom" to describe the essentials of a free society. *Order,* the system of governance; *Justice,* the government's application of the law and asking the question is it there to protect the individual or the power of the state?;

Freedom, the basis and the outcome for all individual activity as protected under the law including entrepreneurship.

> *"Civilization is founded upon order, justice and freedom. All three pillars must be present and balanced for American civilization to endure. Order without freedom is tyranny, Freedom without order is anarchy. And the often contradictory claims of order and freedom are reconciled by justice – those social and political decisions attempting to resolve the competing claims of order and freedom for the good of the people."*
>
> *Source: Seize Freedom by Thaddeus McCotter, 2011*

Modern nations around the world are affected by their political order (structure and leadership) for either advancement or control; the *order* either limits or advances the nation through its impact on justice, and freedom. The application of the *order's* power and policies either supports or limits the conditions necessary for the expansion of knowledge supporting both human and economic development. Societies founded on the integrated principles of order, justice and freedom produce social and economic progress. This is contrary to governmental systems which consolidate power and oppress individuals, and thus limit individual opportunity. Consequently, the freer the society the less power is concentrated in the ideas of interest groups and government and the greater the potential for economic development and social advancement--progress.

Political systems vary and every nation attempts to create systems that reflect its cultural heritage, ideology, and social experience. Each nation develops its form of government based on historical experience, race, religion, culture and, in some instances, social class structures.

In government dominated societies the order is established to preserve the wealth and authority of the powerful. Under this scenario government becomes the means by which the national leaders accumulate great wealth and power. Through propaganda this power structure creates the perception of duty, not freedom to the greater causes of the state. The state creates an image of nationalized power through the greatness of the people by using propaganda to tout the benefits to be derived by all citizens and its enhanced global position. Erstwhile, the government is corrupt and money flows to those at the top, while those at the bottom struggle to survive.

In modern societies that are presumed to be free, the role of government, the *order,* has taken on different obligations. The power of government, as viewed by those in power, is to provide equality, not equal opportunity, through the provision of social benefits. These attempts have either succeeded or failed depending upon the promises made, the level of political corruption, and the success of the programs citizens receive.

In a free society, the three environments of the social, political and economic resemble the following diagram.

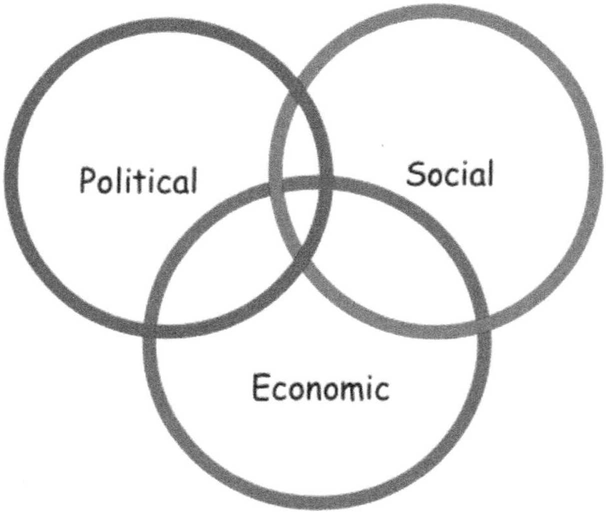

The *non-overlapped* space within each circle reflects the present, the status quo.

When considering the social and economic environments we recognize that they are constantly reacting to the conditions and events of the day; as such, these two environments continuously adjust and vary in size as measured by social needs and wants and using such tools as Gross Domestic Product (GDP), labor participation rates, unemployment and income. For example, in a recession, the economy shrinks and people are laid off having a direct impact on the ability to satisfy individual needs and wants.

During a recession, and depending on political objectives, government may increase spending to support and reduce the economic and income stress of the electorate in its effort to ease recessionary conditions. Government employment, however, remains unchanged, its employment varying little during times of expansion or recession. And, government itself never loses economic resources, or the political motivation to leverage power through the creation of benefit. Government rarely adjusts to real market conditions as it can borrow, spend and tax consistent with its political agenda and obligations.

The area and extent of ***overlap between two circles*** is caused by changes in one or both circles and any affect between them is only temporary producing a non-permanent change.

This temporary effect is reflected in the nation's business cycles. The economy naturally rises and falls based on consumer demand which has a direct impact on employment; jobs are created in an expansion and lost during a recession. It is the expansion/prosperity and recession/contraction of the economy that affects every aspect of society, every social movement and political directive, initiative and policy. For example, during the dot.com boom of 1996 there was great economic growth driven by the investment of private money into the newly developing technology market, the product of speculative money chasing opportunity.

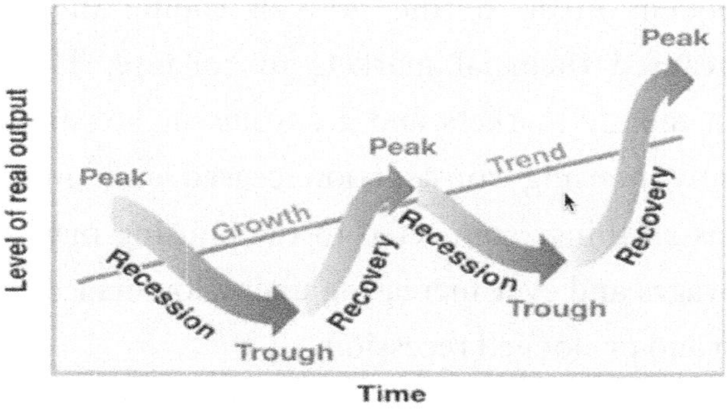

As economies rise, innovative products and ideas create new demand for goods and services--products which expand consumer choices in growing markets. Economic expansion creates the demand for workers with current and relevant knowledge to design, produce and manufacture goods and services. However, when an economy reverses direction, or costs rise to a non-competitive level, companies may not be able to sustain production regardless of worker dedication and skill sets. Overall production is reduced resulting in layoffs and lowered production costs.

In 2007 housing markets were over built, to stimulate demand builders offered incentivized mortgage rates. These rates were offered to induce buyers to purchase homes. But when the incentives expired after a short period of time interest rates reverted to market pricing which the new home buyers could no longer afford to make; consequently they walked away from their homes and obligations. The demand for new homes declined. Homes weren't being sold; bank foreclosures increased and unsold inventory soared. As buyers walked away mortgage payments weren't being received. Investors whom had bought the debt obligations from the banks looked to the insurers of the debt to make them whole.

The subsequent break in the flow of capital in the form of payments caused financial markets to collapse. This created a shortage in money markets and a surplus in housing inventory. Consequently housing construction ceased and unemployment increased as all things connected to the housing markets slowed. With lost wages and ever increasing unemployment the nation fell into a deep and prolonged recession.

In nations around the globe governments try to offset recessionary cycles by spending more on infrastructure and social programs that will stimulate or sustain the economic status quo (Keynesian Economic Theory) with the hope of stabilizing markets and ultimately creating new jobs. The government's goal being to preserve existing employment and support individuals and families by providing essential safety net programs. However, when the government and stimulus and make-work projects end, so do the jobs. Short-term spending creates short-term economic results, temporary spending is intended to reduce the depth of a recession bridging an economy to recovery. To lessen the possibilities of a recession, new political initiatives are considered and launched that will stimulate the economy and address these very complex social and employment problems.

In places where government intervention, taxes and regulations increase costs companies pursue alternative options to remain competitive, including relocation. The purpose of a corporate relocation is to lower all costs; examples of this are companies that leave California or Illinois for Texas or Florida. In today's competitive global marketplace it may not be just leaving one state for another; but it could also include moving to a foreign nation, Mexico or Asia for example. Under such circumstances the desire is to lower all costs across the entire production process, including the hiring of new employees, trained to possess similar skills, and establishing a new--and lower--competitive market price.

The changing needs and wants of consumers, and the global aspects of production, have a direct impact on the demand for skilled and unskilled labor, a shift which further impacts the health and vitality of societies and economies on a global scale. In light of these conditions governments responded by introducing laws and programs designed to protect markets, support employment, and preserve--as much as possible--the production process. To make America more competitive, in 2017, President Trump and the Congress passed laws that reduced taxes. Furthermore, the Administration instituted a review of all regulations requiring that any new regulation be accompanied by the elimination of at least two regulations for every significant new one, and to keep the net new costs at zero. The combination produced an expansion of employment, an increase in consumer demand, rising wages, increasing home values, new corporate investment, and an increase in wealth across the nation.

The ***overlap*** of the three circles produces progress.

The goal of every nation is to succeed, for whatever reason, whether it is social, economic or political in its nature. To accomplish this all three circles must work together, each reacting to the needs of the other. A growing and successful economy doesn't require constant stimulus, government spending, but it does require spending in the right places with the view that government's purpose is to serve the needs of the people and the economy and not just its own political advantage. It requires investing in the right infrastructure, in people as well as in the ground. It requires the proper motivations and the highest order thinking as previously described by Dale Ahlquist.

Power vs. Risk Curve

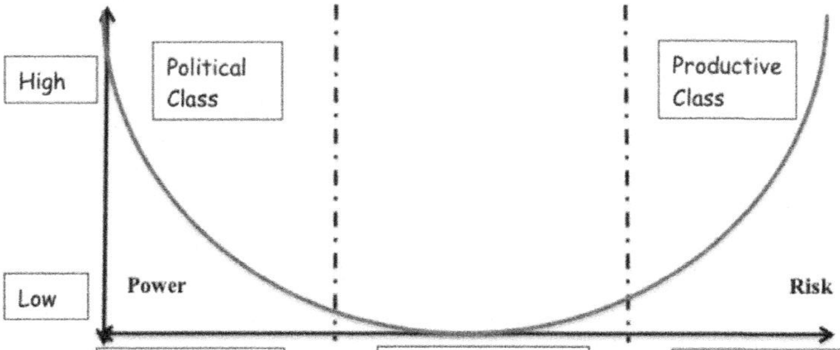

Government has:
1. Political, regulatory & taxing authority
2. Power to identify needs & legislate programs
3. Owns no risk, risk is transferred to tax payers.

Beneficiaries:
1. 49% of Americans receive some form of government benefit
2. Elderly and disabled receive 60% of these benefits
3. Citizens will vote to sustain or gain benefit based upon real or perceived need.
4. Citizen's experience reduced personal risk, exchanging risk for benefit.

People & Companies:
1. Only people and companies create and own risk
2. Risk is applied to capital and productive resources.
3. Generates and Produces income
4. 100% of people and businesses must comply with regulations
5. The greater the risk the greater the probability of success or failure.

PART III

THE FUNDAMENTALS

ESSENTIAL # 3: ADVANCING THE REQUISITES

7

THE REQUISITES, ESSENTIAL TO ADVANCE AND SUCCEED

To be successful and to compete in the world a nation must have and apply all of the following essential elements, without these competitive political ideas, economic innovations and social advancement, progress, cannot occur. These are not necessarily in hierarchical order but all must be present for any nation to succeed:

1. An educated populace,
2. Diverse income levels,
3. Entrepreneurial risk and leadership,
4. Asset ownership,
5. Investor capital,
6. Access to financing,
7. A diverse economic structure,
8. Competitive product markets,
9. Manufacturing and technological development,

10. Innovative products that meet the needs of local and global markets,
11. A global communication and transportation network,
12. Expansive consumer markets,
13. A representative government(s),
14. A competitive political system,
15. An established and accepted legal system.

In the 1990s China studied the outcomes of its 1978 economic and agricultural reforms, and based on these results, determined that additional changes were necessary to continue to grow its economy. These reforms began with the de-collectivization of China's agriculture and the implementation of market reforms in the production of food which would ultimately lead to major changes throughout China's consumer and industrial markets. These changes not only included selling off government owned businesses and industries, but reforming the entire economic system by reducing the government's direct involvement and control. These reforms advanced slowly during the 1980s but took on added importance following the collapse of the Soviet Union in 1989 when China recognized that if it didn't change its economic system, it too would follow the path of the Soviet Union and the demise of its own political system.

By 1997 China was in economic decline. Seeing the future and considering its options it decided to modify its economic system; this decision produced today's international powerhouse. However, to complete this economic transformation will require a change to its political system, including greater political freedom for its citizens and a reduction in the corruption of its local political leaders and government officials. Not only must there be a willingness by leaders to relinquish power but there must also be a complimentary understanding of the workings of a free society. This requires that leaders advance the needs of the people ahead of their own political power and agendas. Without these internal changes China will gradually slow and lose whatever economic advantage it currently holds in the competitive global market place.

To-date, China's political leaders have been reluctant to take this next step as it requires a willingness to relinquish power and grant a subsequent transfer of power to the people. However, China's leaders recently adopted a more traditional centralized power position by naming President Xi as President for Life. This necessitated a change to the Chinese Constitution removing the two term limit for Chinese Presidents. This act alone demonstrated the enormous political power held by Xi. Effectively Xi leveraged his political power and elevated his status to the level of Chairman Mao, the founder of Communist China.

Begging the question: Can they, are they, prepared to self-govern?

The social, economic and political environments exist in juxtaposition to each other creating a natural tension common to all societies, and the nations that manage these best will advance the most. This requires that the populace of any nation be capable of self-governance, often an incorrect assumption, and one that many democracies have of lesser developed countries. In a free society it is this tension that creates solutions to complex social, economic and political problems.

Mexico appears to have all of the elements essential for success as a competitive modern nation: ample natural resources combined with the freedom to pursue social advancement and economic success. Combined this should lead to the development of a society that creates wealth and opportunity. However, Mexico's government is corrupt, often unable or unwilling to provide for the safety of its citizens. It has a political system impacted by corruption and which has come at a great cost to its citizen's social and economic advancement. In addition, its government has failed to exert effective control over its criminal elements. As a result Mexico doesn't provide a safe environment in which its citizens can prosper. Consequently, its government's very nature becomes destructive of its cultural fabric; it fails to provide the most basic needs of education, security and opportunity. Consequently, it establishes the conditions that limit or prevent economic growth and social development.

In light of these conditions, and its ever growing population, its citizens have but one option--or release valve--to leave the country through either legal or illegal immigration to nations that provide the essential elements of safety and prosperity. In this case the most convenient destination is the United States.

There are other countries that have the same struggle with the different underlying conditions. Greece, for example, has a homogenous population with a single social ideology. However, its government has over reached; it struggles to deliver on its political promises: the continuation of social benefits to an ever expectant population. Today, Greeks demand more benefits than the nation can afford to provide. The nation is, for all practical purposes, bankrupt with the need to redefine the social contract between the government and its citizens. Compounding this is its relationship with the European Union, of which it is a member and an indebted borrower. The combination of these factors have produced political uncertainty and a constant demand for political change that could deliver the benefits promised by prior regimes and programs, even though these cannot be sustained economically.

For free societies and nations to succeed requires the political ideas proposed by John Locke, Thomas Jefferson and so many others beginning more than 200 years ago. First, for long term success, a nation and its government must be responsible to its citizens. Second, citizens must be responsible for their own economic success however that may be defined. Third, citizens must treat their government with great cynicism in order to restrict and limit the power of their government.

A government's function is defined by its role of protecting the public safety (defense) and the provision of whatever safety nets it deems necessary. The social benefits flowing from this, though, are judged differently by every society. Thus, the social benefits derived by the populace varies as does the cost and efficacy of delivery. Government programs must have value to *all* citizens (education, safety net programs, healthcare, social security), with benefits that are accessible to all, and, depending on the need, they must be economically *affordable*.

In the process of delivering programs, governments move from the idea of economic freedom and entrepreneurship to the concept of regulation and economic security especially where social benefits become the greater part of government spending. Benefits should be accessed based on need rather than becoming a permanent part of the social contract. In the event that the defense of the nation and the social contract are not achievable, the competition between nations will ultimately decide winners and losers, consistent with the experiences of Mexico, Greece and, perhaps, America with its ever increasing debt burden.

The following diagram illustrates the tensions that exist between the power of government and the freedom of individuals.

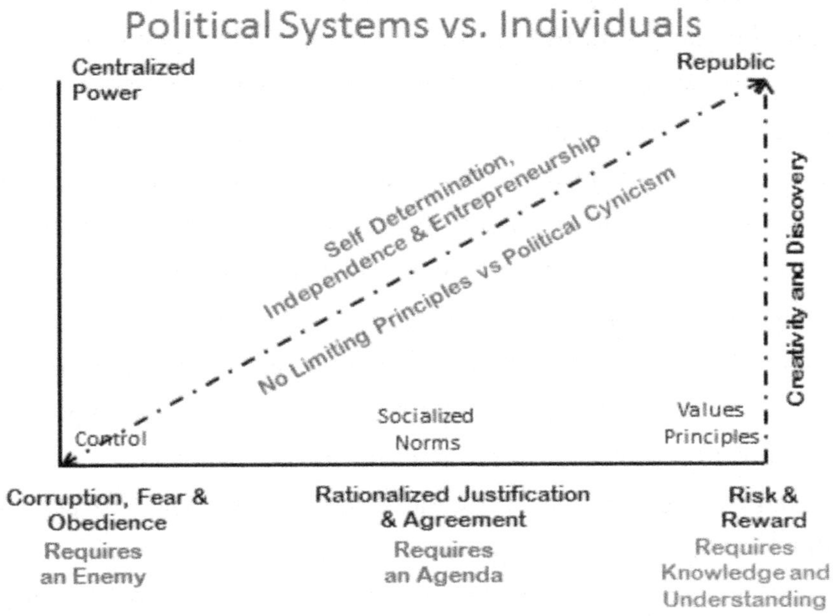

In Japan the modern political order was established following World War II: a parliamentary system that created a high cost, high social benefit system based on the necessity of the times, and a model of lifetime employment. Today's consequence is a moribund economy tied to a social benefit system and high taxes. Japan's national debt currently sits at 200+ percent of its GDP, and growing. Government borrowing, even at today's low rates, forces out consumer and small business credit in the national credit marketplace, reducing the ability to satisfying the needs and wants of the individual and small businesses.

> **"*GOVERNMENT POLICY IMPACTS CONSUMER LENDING***
>
> *Consumer lending in Japan is likely to be influenced by the increase in the VAT(Value Added Tax) scheduled for the early part of the forecast period. Following his re-election as leader of the ruling Liberal Democratic Party, September 2018, Prime Minister Shinzo Abe announced that the VAT hike would go ahead as planned in October 2019.*
>
> ***NEGATIVE INTEREST WEAKENS MORTGAGES/HOUSING LENDING***
>
> *In January 2018, the Bank of Japan decided to maintain the negative interest policy it initially introduced in 2016, continuing with an interest rate of -0.1 percent, despite concerns amongst some economists that the policy could lead to speculation and bubbles, and that low-cost liquidity would not help to revitalize the economy in the aftermath of a bubble burst.*
>
> *~Consumer Lending in Japan, EuroMonitor International, November 2018*

Financing for Japan's global corporations is no longer accomplished through local markets, but rather through the international money markets, reflecting the global nature of business and the fungible aspects of money. And, as corporations have become global, its home money markets have also become less relevant. As a result, the competition for money between the national government, small business and consumers, has had a restrictive impact on the growth of the economy.

Caught between Japan's increasing tax rates and global money markets the home market economy has remained stagnant. This is especially so given the nation's frugal spending habits as reported by the Nikkei Asian Review, January 2019. Economic growth and success in Japan's home market is limited given its inability to stimulate market demand, financial competition and its limited natural resources. The result is a nation that is politically and historically inward looking, with reduced access to money markets for local and small business investment and expansion, and a steady-state large corporate national strategy.

Japan's social construct has also evolved slowly, not rapidly changing nor expanding. Japan's current population growth rate is a negative .25 percent. Culturally the nation has a homogenous population that doesn't openly welcome immigrants; as such the population is aging with a median age of 44.8 years and a median education level of 15 years. (Japan, CIA Fact Book, 2010.)

Japan's economy has struggled. The last decade has been called "the lost decade." It has struggled with an anemic economy, high taxes and slow consumer spending. Low interest rates have failed to stimulate the economy even though Japan has one of the most significantly developed industrial complexes. However, the burden of taxation, public benefit programs and an aging population has limited its economic vitality. Given its level of economic development, the traditional use of Keynesian Economics, and the use of government spending and taxation to stimulate or contract the economy, has failed to produce positive results. Given this cost burden, Japanese companies, like many American manufacturers, have sought the advantage of investing, expanding and outsourcing in other less costly markets such as China, Vietnam, and Mexico, in order to lower costs and remain competitive. As Japanese corporations relocated to take advantage of developing and expanding economies, these nations, among many others, benefited from the expansions and the subsequent new jobs due to the rising costs of doing business in Japan. The end result is that Japan is losing economic vitality and jobs to other countries.

Inertia: A body in motion stays in motion until acted upon by an outside force.

The path which many nations find themselves on is not only historical but reflective of their culture, social experience, expectations and national traditions. The combination of these has often impacted economic opportunity and sustained a political experience developed over generations. As is so often the case, history itself leads to the present and prevents nations from capitalizing on the change opportunity. Under these circumstances it is change that arrives, yet was never sought, thrust upon the people of a nation as a result of unanticipated events. An example are the nations around the world that were devastated by World War II. When everything was destroyed it not only took a national effort but also one supported internationally to achieve some semblance of national, social and economic recovery.

Even when cultures recognize their limitations, they accept the conditions present in their circumstance, as any effort to advance change or oppose the present entails assuming personal risk. Economics is even more difficult to change when there is no culture of discovery and market opportunities are limited, but which people seek out; and which beckons when the present is no longer acceptable. Under these circumstances people will naturally, if not grudgingly, abandon their present situation to migrate to another community or nation, seeking opportunities not available in their present circumstance.

Likewise, politics is perhaps more difficult to modify and change. Societies accept the politics of the present order, as processes are understood, known and accepted as: "*better the devil you know than the devil you don't.*" Societies may not be willing to accept political faults and tyranny, but citizens are also less willing to risk change as they may be unable to control or predict the outcome. Consequently, a natural resistance arises as the threat to today's circumstance, individual power and benefit are considered. People then prefer to preserve the known system as the unknown outcome of change threatens the present, and the risks perhaps, too high. Regardless of the system in place, a nation's direction is near impossible to change, modify or recreate.

Throughout history the impacts on the social, economic and political environments are linked in a causal system, with singular events and advancements created by individuals that have far reaching consequence. The relationship between these environments is relative and dependent upon the political system in place (capitalism, monarchy, theocracy, fascism or communism). The outcomes of the latter four may be the consequences of monarchs, dictators or totalitarian governments in which power is vested in one or a few leaders (oligopoly) that retain power and control over a nation and its people. In today's modern world all five systems may use a parliament, or congress, to either advance the needs of a free society *or* affirm the political will of the powerful within a fear society.

The *present*, then, is a result of policy decisions made in the past, with their consequences reflected in current social and economic conditions. In evaluating a nation's present day conditions, it is essential to examine the motives and interactions of individuals and their decisions to determine the impacts on the political and economic environments. The objective is to demonstrate the linkage between social behaviors in the aggregate, and the resultant political and economic event(s) that impact society in its entirety.

The following table lists the essentials for a modern society; each aspect is dependent upon the events, leadership and success in the other two.

Measuring Society

1. Social stability	1. Unsatisfied needs and wants, competitive markets	1. A government responsive to the needs of the people.
2. Entrepreneurial Risk	2. Risk based Innovation	2. A competitive and reactive political system that serves and supports the needs of the people and the economic system.
3. Education => Knowledge	3. Intellectual capital	3. A diverse educated populace with ample job opportunities.
4. Intellectual curiosity & inquiry. Creativity	4. Labor (skilled & unskilled)	4. An innovative and reactive political system serving the needs of the people and business.
5. Markets for goods & services	5. Capital; affordable & productive (money & equipment)	5. Preserves access to capital and risk.
6. Work and income opportunities	6. Global Communications and Information	6. Regulations which create and promote a safe working environment
7. Limited labor un-rest	7. Applied Energy	7. Protects natural assets and access to productive natural resources and the environment
8. Low Unemployment	8. Established Markets (local, national & global)	8. The will to correct political/ social problems
9. Modern societies are impacted negatively by high unemployment rates.	9. Globally recognized & accepted products, e.g. Cell Phones	9. Effective oversight of government by institutions and citizens
10. Cultural diversity	10. Productive use of land	

8

THE SOCIAL TENSIONS

A society is ultimately judged and measured by how well its political system treats its own citizens; the most crucial aspect is the establishment of a judicial process founded on the principles and preservation of individual rights. A just society is most likely to succeed in the long term if it builds a legal system which protects civil liberties and the rights of its citizens. This includes the right to own property in whatever form that may take, and the rights of the accused from the unrestrained power of the government. A system that protects the rights of the individual and all of the nation's citizens, and which is acknowledged in constitutional law. This is a legal system that applies to all citizens and constrains the power of the government, and it is a legal system which preserves individual freedom and protects the individual. However, time is required to develop such a system and apply its principles through a fair and established system of rules and laws that are learned and respected.

Today, we have moved beyond just the consideration of material property and criminal law. We recognize an individual's civil liberties and, more importantly, man's creative, intellectual rights. Thomas Paine in his essay, *The Rights of Man,* provided a clear definition of these rights. His definition remains relevant in its application today, in both context and practice.

> *"... consider the civil rights of man... Man did not enter into society to become worse than he was before, nor to have fewer rights than he had before, but to have those rights better secured. His natural rights are the foundation of all his civil rights. But in order to pursue this distinction with more precision, it will be necessary to mark the different qualities of natural and civil rights.*
>
> *A few words will explain this. Natural rights are those which appertain to man in right of his existence. Of this kind are all the intellectual rights, or rights of the mind, and also all those rights of acting as an individual for his own comfort and happiness, which are not injurious to the natural rights of others. Civil rights are those which appertain to man in right of his being a member of society. Every civil right has for its foundation in some natural right pre-existing in the individual, but to the enjoyment of which his individual power is not, in all cases, sufficiently competent."*
>
> *-Thomas Paine, 'The Rights of Man'*

This definition of individual rights, however, isn't recognized and honored in all cases especially when applied to totalitarian governments, absolute monarchies, theocracies and extreme socialist political systems. These systems reserve the rights and power to the state, establishing the power of government at its core, and placing individual rights second to the needs of the state and the wants of its political class.

The outcome is a system in which the state reserves all power to itself, and by extension, controls society and the economic system for its own benefit.

Rather than protect and preserve the natural rights of the individual, these governments usurp the most basic human rights in favor of the state's power; taken from, and not granted by, the citizen.

When considering modern societies the following criteria apply and must be considered in the understanding of how modern societies function and react in their social interactions.

1. Social stability
2. Cultural diversity
3. Moral behavior
4. Education + Experience => Knowledge
5. Intellectual Curiosity and Creativity
6. Work and income opportunities
7. Markets for goods & services
8. Limited labor unrest
9. Low Unemployment
10. The will to correct political/social problems
11. Intellectual curiosity & inquiry.

12. All societies are impacted negatively by high unemployment rates.

Social stability

1. Complex social conditions exist in every community. These included such variables as: location, heritage, religion, education levels, income, risk, skill levels, employment opportunities, natural resources, the historical economic base, the entrepreneurial spirit of its citizens, political stability or instability, external conditions, threats to self, etc.
2. A practiced moral behavior exercised by members of society to the benefit of all.
3. Cultural diversity in communities causes change which directly impacts a community, changes which often produce unexpected outcomes including the introduction of new goods and ideas expanding markets, creating new opportunities, and jobs. It produces a cultural expansion which satisfies and creates new tastes and opportunities in all aspects of community life; it can also cause conflict or flight. Regardless of the outcomes its impact will change existing lifestyles in any community over time.
4. The age and vitality of the population can also cause change, for example, an elderly community while stable is a relatively non-expanding established community which consumes fewer goods, versus an expanding

younger population which creates and demands new opportunities and attracts younger residents and workers.

5. In a Republic, citizens grant political power and authority to elected officials. However, this authority may be ineffective when other conditions are present and may cause instability, these include: high levels of crime, political corruption, limited educational advancement, and poor economic conditions.
6. For new immigrants a paradigm shift is required as social and economic conditions warrant new practices. So as needs and wants become apparent the demand for a new "learned" experience is critical to the adoption of traditions, education, the accepted/expected social behavior (Mores). Furthermore, the need to apply skills and earn wages, the obligations associated with debt, entrepreneurship and the required taxation. For these the adoption of new national traditions, a new language, the pursuit educational opportunities, and the understanding of individual rights and legal practices can take up to two generations.
7. The political and social history of immigrants has a direct impact on a community's values and core beliefs; a positive impact is created when immigrants are welcomed; an opposite impact is created ***if*** the new immigrants are not welcomed and not incorporated into the larger citizenry and are forced to remain separate by the community at large; or by the choice of the immigrant to remain separate.

Cultural diversity

1. Immigration (legal and illegal) expands the cultural diversity in the near long term adding value and complexity to the culture and society. However, *if* distinct core values exist or are present within the new groups this can create social conflict and prejudices. Internal conflict reduces social and economic interactions and reduces opportunities for the entire community.
2. Cultural conflicts can arise between existing residents and new immigrants if the newly arrived are forced to remain separate and not welcomed and incorporated into the society. Or the reverse, if the immigrant chooses to not participate in the local, state and national economic and political scene then the benefit to the community is lost.

Low Unemployment

Social problems decrease in expanding economies as income levels rise, unemployment decreases and social problems lessen.

In an expanding economy new knowledge and labor skill sets are demanded and developed, which cause an expansion in demand for goods and services creating new opportunities.

. . .

Societies are impacted negatively by high unemployment rates.

1. High unemployment creates a surplus of workers in the labor force resulting in higher competition for existing and available jobs. A labor surplus produces downward pressure on wages, and increases competition between workers for available jobs, producing a decline in worker demand.
2. In a shrinking economy social problems increase and attract political attention with the expectation that community problems and issues can be addressed. So often the expectation is that by creating new policies and social programs solutions will be found rather than exploring ways to transform the underlying economic conditions.

Education => Knowledge & intellectual curiosity & inquiry.

1. The success of any society is linked to the education level of its citizens, and the application of their knowledge in the pursuit of personal gain and advancement.
2. Many lower income Americans have not benefited from the educational opportunities present in America resulting in lower lifetime earnings and a reduced quality of life.

The *will* to correct political/social problems

1. When social problems are not addressed through either social action or effective political processes the advancement of society starts to slow potentially developing fractures within the greater community. The unity necessary to solve common problems and create solutions is weakened or stalled.
2. When social/political change is not advanced nor demanded by society then stagnation sets in. If no action is taken by the social or political institutions then present problems remain unchallenged and unresolved. Politicians, even if they are aware of the need are not necessarily desirous of change as it may threaten existing power relationships, for example the power of the white majority in the South following the American Civil War.
3. A Society's advancement is fully dependent upon the system of justice in place, a system which must protect individual freedoms and rights if the society is to advance. In the United States, the Constitution's "Bill of Rights" was incorporated to protect the freedom of individuals from the actions of the state and from other's who might try to limit by definition those freedoms. However, these protections can be ignored by the politically powerful and legal system if it goes counter to their political power and objectives.
4. As America has evolved the Constitution's original

applications and interpretations have expanded through both new laws and rulings to fit the needs of an evolving society. Today Americans look to the courts to be the final arbiter, to legalize and correct perceived and real injustices, and has become the preferred process to redefine acceptable social behavior.

5. Beware the willingness of those that self-declare themselves as "tolerant," these are the first to attempt to limit the speech of those who question the intolerance of the supposed tolerant.

Markets for goods & services

1. An expanding economy creates new ideas and businesses which advances the community overall.
2. In an expanding market entrepreneurial drive is elevated creating new employment opportunities, opportunities leveraged against knowledge and experience for greater personal economic benefit.

Work and income opportunities

People move throughout America, as well as come to it, seeking a better standard of living and quality of life than their former home could offer.

Personal improvement and benefit are the drivers of this new quality of life.

. . .

Outcomes:

If effective solutions are not sought that resolve social issues, or if politicians don't address them, the possibility exists that extreme negative reactions will result; consequences range from dissatisfaction with political/elected officials to mob actions and chaos. Modern day examples of the latter include riots in Greece, Egypt, and rebellion/revolution and civil war in Syria. Historical examples include the worst case scenarios of the French and Russian Revolutions in which political and social instability persisted over time and at great cost in lives, productivity and the destruction of previously existing social traditions and contracts, productive economic structures and wealth.

9

THE ECONOMIC TENSIONS

MEASURING AN EFFECTIVE ECONOMY

Every place throughout the world people live and exchange value to satisfy the most basic of human needs. In this exchange a mutual benefit is established that satisfies the needs and wants of the parties involved. The process of satisfying our wants through a mutually beneficial transaction produces the conditions necessary to sustain an economy, regardless of location and value. An economy can exist in the most rudimentary conditions and can function in a legal or illegal marketplace.

In the competitive international marketplace an economy must grow, expand and satisfy not only the needs of its people, it must be in a position to reach beyond its borders to sell and acquire the goods and services available around the world. To compete societies require the delivery of goods and services produced in competitive international markets and which complement the creativity and entrepreneurship of its own citizens. To accomplish this knowledge and motivated self-interest are transformed through the leveraging and creative use of innovation, capital, market competition and the motivations of a nation's risk takers. A market economy's ability to expand and grow is the product of this capitalism; it unleashes the intellectual and entrepreneurial drive of people.

This expansion is dependent upon the risk and creativity of individuals; and it flourishes best when the political "order' and "justice" system are restrained and protect the ideas that advance an economy. To achieve growth the "freedom" of the market must be supported and protected by the political system, it accomplishes this by limiting taxes and regulations or incenting the entrepreneurial spirit of the nation. Depending on the methodology and objectives, politics and power will either restrict or support the economy. A fact understood by every Industrialist, Economic Development professional, Banker and Investor around the world. If supported the market responds by increasing the supply of goods and services and producing new and expanding payrolls.

Discovery, innovation, risk and investment are present in every economy and their availability either expands or contracts the economy. Expansion and growth, however, of economies only occurs when an investment in productive resources is made creating new supply, demand and employment. This physical and intellectual investment of capital measures the market opportunity and the risk that entrepreneurs and businesses are willing to take in response to opportunities.

Furthermore, based upon a community's size, its entrepreneurship, its access to capital and its economic diversity produce a more complex economic base. This, in turn, creates greater prosperity for all citizens. These ideas were confirmed by research performed by Lay Gibson and Marshall Worden at the University of Arizona in their study Estimating the Base Economic Multiplier in 1981; this study showed that the more diverse and productive the economy the greater the economic multiplier, the result: more job opportunities. While an evaluative study of local economies on the micro level, the impact translates directly to the larger macro economy. The outcome: Greater economic benefit to the individual, community, state and nation.

> *"So that the record of history is absolutely crystal clear. There is no alternative way, so far discovered, of improving the lot of the ordinary people that can hold a candle to the productive activities that are unleashed by a free enterprise system."*
>
> *~Milton Friedman*

For a society to advance, there exists qualitative and quantitative essentials which produce a Modern Economy, these include:

1. Unsatisfied needs and wants
2. Entrepreneurial leadership and Risk
3. Intellectual capital
4. Land
5. Labor (skilled & unskilled)
6. Investment capital and affordable and productive money and equipment

7. Energy, distributed and reliable
8. Global Information
9. Global Communications and transportation systems
10. An economy which creates and deploys readily available technology
11. Markets (local, national & global)
12. Globally recognized & accepted products
13. In a global market excessive taxes and regulation will cause manufacturers to consider alternative locations with lower production costs
14. High interest rates and inflation cause harm to the economy

Excessive taxes and regulation will cause manufacturers to consider alternative locations with lower production costs.

1. Government has a direct impact on the economy of any community, state or nation. The greater the involvement of government, while it may have a desired effect on social issues policy, it can have a significant impact on the growth and viability of the economy as a result of higher taxes and regulation.
2. For small cities governmental leadership and regulations are a major factor in the creation of, or barrier to, new employment and an expanding tax base.
3. State or provincial governments provide the basic foundation for economic development by self-managing the desire for regulation and taxation; a difficult thing to

accomplish when political issues arise. State or provincial governments *will* either support or hinder economic growth as its actions have a direct impact on the present and future prosperity of residents.

4. Likewise, the national power of the government has the ability to fully support, restrict or destroy economic entrepreneurship. The greater the concentration of power in the central government the less effective its state, provincial and local economies are. This concept especially applies to developing nations where money, power and control are concentrated in a few cities. Examples include Mexico City, Beijing, Moscow and Paris.

Entrepreneurial Leadership & Risk, New ideas and Intellectual capital

1. When knowledge, creativity, innovation, and investment are applied they produce new business, work opportunities and income. These are all products of entrepreneurship and risk.

Land, Labor (skilled and unskilled), Capital, affordable & productive (money, equipment and technology), Energy, Global Communications and Transportation Systems, Global Information, Markets (local, national and global).

1. Economic innovation creates new technologies which impact competition which produces even more innovation and consumer products. Increased demand and competition for goods and services places downward pressure on prices and forces improvements in productivity. It increases competition for differentiated products and alternative pricing strategies; which in turn, creates greater demand for workers at all skill levels.
2. Large investor owned capital is globally portable, it seeks a risk that is based on an evaluated opportunity and its potential for gain.
3. Small capital, or savings, tends to be risk averse and is typically invested in local productive resources through the banking system.
4. Entrepreneurs and companies will determine investment strategies and make spending decisions based upon operating structures, costs and perceived market opportunities in which present and future risk are analyzed in the context of market conditions.
5. The more diverse and complex a nation's economic system the greater and more complex its infrastructure needs are. Government's role is to support developing and expanding economies by providing the common infrastructure essential to the advancement of the economy by providing the means for the movement of people, goods and services.

Globally recognized and accepted products,

Complex economies include direct and indirect support for: private and alternative forms of ownership, new science, financing, manufacturing, deployed technologies, resource and component suppliers, services, transportation systems, construction, abundant as well as diverse power and energy resources, international trade, access to natural resources, agriculture and the stewardship of the natural environment.

Unsatisfied needs and wants

A large and growing middle-income population creates an expanding marketplace with greater demand for goods and services; a declining middle-income population reduces market choices.

The combination and support for these criteria results in the creation of individual wealth and economic power, failure to do so will produce a stagnant non-advancing society.

Outcomes:

An economy relies upon present circumstance and market conditions which include: workers skills and the availability of goods and services. All economies leverage existing systems and production techniques which benefit from, and react to, new inputs, including: innovation, evolutionary and unexpected

Surprise, supply and demand, the availability of capital, and the stability and predictability of market conditions and political direction.

Under these circumstances money is the primary productive resource and motivator of any economy; it is measured, it is risk oriented, it is profit driven and it is portable; it seeks opportunities based on the safety and predictability of market conditions and safe harbors. It is a tool of the powerful and their associated wannabes. It is the single most important driver of corruption and illegal activity, and, it is the greatest motivator for innovation and the creation of wealth. It can be deployed for productive purposes, consumption and good works.

Consistent with the above, money reacts negatively to uncertainty and the political restraint of economic growth and success. Political dysfunction, corruption and other criminal and economic constraints on entrepreneurship and money reduce and limit the investment of new capital, deterring social and economic progress. To counter this, and to protect business interest, business leaders can, and will, pursue the development of political influence.

Failure to protect property rights and the accumulation of wealth creates an impact which reaches beyond the economy itself, reflected in the reduction and decline of social and economic liberties. If rights and property in all its forms are not protected power is concentrated in the hands of the political system which produces a shift from the rights of the individual to the perceived good of the masses; Socialism and perhaps the ultimate prohibition of rights; Totalitarianism. The result is a process which consolidates power in the hands of the government and its institutions, a power destructive of risk and competition, social liberty and advancement, opportunity and creativity.

"Suppose a nation, rich and poor, high and low, ten millions in number, all assembled together; not more than one or two millions will have lands, houses, or any personal property; if we take into the account the women and children, or even if we leave them out of the question, a great majority of every nation is wholly destitute of property, except a small quantity of clothes, and a few trifles of other movables. Would Mr. Nedham be responsible that, if all were to be decided by a vote of the majority, the eight or nine millions who have no property, would not think of usurping over the rights of the one or two millions who have? Property is surely a right of mankind as really as liberty. Perhaps, at first, prejudice, habit, shame or fear, principle or religion, would restrain the poor from attacking the rich, and the idle from usurping on the industrious; but the time would not be long before courage and enterprise would come, and pretexts be invented by degrees, to countenance the majority in dividing all the property among them, or at least, in sharing it equally with its present possessors. Debts would be abolished first; taxes laid heavy on the rich, and not at all on the others; and at last a downright equal division of everything be demanded, and voted. What would be the consequence of this? The idle, the vicious, the intemperate, would rush into the utmost extravagance of debauchery, sell and spend all their share, and then demand a new division of those who purchased from them. The moment the idea is admitted into society, that property is not as sacred as the laws of God, and that there is not a force of law and public

justice to protect it, anarchy and tyranny commence. If "Thou shalt not covet," and "Thou shalt not steal," were not commandments of Heaven, they must be made inviolable precepts in every society, before it can be civilized or made free."

~John Adams, "In Defence of the Constitution of the United States; In recognition of the value of ownership and property rights."

10

POLITICAL TENSIONS

"Elected parliaments, habeas corpus, free contract, equality before the law, open markets, an unrestricted press, the right to proselytize for any religion, jury trials: these things are not somehow the natural condition of an advanced society. They are specific products of a political ideology developed in the language in which you are reading these words. The fact that those ideas, and that language, have become so widespread can make us lose sight of how exceptional they were in origin."

~Daniel Hannan, "Inventing Freedom: How the English-Speaking Peoples Made the Modern World"

How the Political Environment is evaluated.

There have been no new, successful ideas in government since the writing of the US Constitution. Government remains the battleground between the power of the politician, the role of bureaucracies and the independence of the individual. This is a conflict that will not be solved in our lifetime, however, promises will still be made and people will still remain hopeful. Throughout the world *bad* government is more the norm than the exception; it remains the motivator of immigrants, power struggles, war and death.

As a consequence, and subject to the political *order* in place, the system either supports the power of the government, or the freedom of the individual. And, through the political system in place, it will either leverage this established "*order* to its own benefit or the individual's right to be free. Determining the balance between these two competing forces is the greatest challenge faced by every free society. Through this order, governments determine the conditions that create a nation's ability to thrive; and, subject to its propensity to restrict, protect or expand an individual's personal freedom, it will determine the future success or failure of its people.

There has been much thought and writing on this subject; however, at the end of the day the very principles and ideas created in the past have not changed. The only real variable is which direction will government take, and how will it influence human conditions and outcomes. The application and use of its power, in whatever form it takes, will establish and pre-determine whether a people will be free to prosper or be oppressed and possessing limited opportunity.

In some countries the political system is a function of a power oriented government ideology and the ensuing bureaucratic corruption, all in the name of serving the public good. It creates wealth and power for select individuals and, in the process, limits the freedom of the rest of society. This is evident around the world where people flee their home countries, migrating in search of personal safety and the pursuit of opportunity. It is interesting that we never hear of people rushing towards dictatorships or corrupt governments.

> *"The truth is that all men having power ought to be mistrusted."*
>
> *~James Madison, Founding Father, Author of the Constitution, 4th President of the United States.*

In sharp contrast, a nation with stable government, abundant knowledge and innovative entrepreneurs, competing political ideas can complement the social and economic structure; expanding personal freedom, knowledge and creativity which produces progress and allows the opportunity desired by so many around the world.

The essentials of a modern government include:

1. A government responsive to the needs of the people.

2. A competitive political system that serves and supports the needs of the people and their economic system.
3. A diverse educated populace with ample job opportunities.
4. An innovative political system serving the needs of all people and business, with regulations that create a safe working environment.
5. A constrained political system that preserves capital, and provides access to productive resources.

A government responsive to the needs of the people and the economy.

1. In a free society, government's primary responsibility is to protect the intellectual and property rights of its citizens.
2. Government's secondary responsibility is to provide for a communities safety and the nation's defense, however that may be defined.
3. The larger the nation the more difficult it is to serve the needs of a diverse and complex society. Representative governments can be engulfed by the winds of political change, and lose sight of their stated purpose.
4. Bureaucracies can be both political in their nature and methodical in serving their citizens.
5. Local governments are the most responsive as these are the closest to voters, the more distant from the voter

base the more politicians are subject to the pressures of special interest.

A political system that preserves capital and provides access to productive resources.

1. Government's responsibility to the economy is to preserve this expression of knowledge and market freedom. Government can tax and regulate, but over-regulation and taxation depletes the economy of its risk-oriented energy.
2. Government serves the community when it provides for the effective and safe use of public and private infrastructure.
3. To have a vibrant economic environment government must provide the conditions and regulations that preserve the wilingness to assume risk, preserve competition, and protect the pursuit of profitability in the market. To do otherwise undermines the vitality of the economic system restricting its innovation and burdening its stability.

A competitive political system that serves and supports the needs of the people and their economic system.

1. The competition in political ideas occurs when a

political system guarantees individual freedom and has sufficient social and economic power to pursue and support alternate positions. Competing interests are evident in the political processes that support specific agendas, achieved through influence and the pursuit of specific goals. These interests possess alternate goals; agendas which may be promoted under the guise of progress and the protection of individual rights.

2. Through the imposition of taxes, regulation and control government exerts enormous power over an economy; its regulatory processes directly impact a nation's ability to produce goods and services which can either expand opportunity or destroy the lives and economic resources of its citizens. Seeking a balance in solving or evolving an economy is a challenging task for all politicians and bureaucracies.
3. In a nation where government is viewed as a profession it creates a "political class" which has the power to influence the direction and acts of government. Lifetime politicians and permanent government employees produce more power for themselves when they defend the *to serve* proposition. This condition results in the passage of new laws and the creation of new regulations that support philosophies intended to create a *better* or *more* equal society at the expense of culture, tax payers or the economy in general. While a professional and permanent civil service is necessary and less subject to the influences of elected politicians it is equally important to recognize the positive and negative impacts of its actions on the lives of the nation's citizens.

4. The political class maintains a separate condition which individuals in other employment sectors don't possess, that is, they take no employment risk, and their jobs are for the most part permanent. While defined as Civil Servants they serve the government and its political agenda. And, as long as they serve this master well their positions and jobs are never at risk. A distinction that applies to only a few other natural business monopolies.
5. In a competitive world, governments compete directly with each other not through military might but through the strength and vitality of their economies. Often-times foreign governments offer direct or indirect incentives to corporations and individuals simply by ***not*** imposing parallel taxes and regulations.

As a consequence, for societies to remain free, nations are inextricably linked to the percentage of active and knowledgeable voters that make critical choices in primaries and general elections; a process designed to preserve freedoms and resolve social issues as well as political conflict. But the greater the power concentrated in government's hands the more difficult it is to protect the rights of the individual or the entrepreneurship of the market place. The power of government easily becomes unrestricted rather than limited in its application.

Outcomes:

If representative government retains the correct focus of

serving its citizens, good government can be the product. However today, all countries have constitutions, pass laws that can be interpreted, enforced or ignored based on the political philosophies of the day. For example, many drug laws that relate to marijuana are now being ignored as it is rapidly becoming a newly decriminalized substance. This is a drug that has both a legal and illegal marketplace; it is sold in regulated stores as well as by unregulated individuals on the street. Regardless of the source, there is a benefit to be gained by the politicians—a new tax source; the seller/buyer, a differentiated price and cost, and perhaps society as a beneficiary of reduced costs in enforcement and prosecution.

Politics and governance is further complicated when politicians enter office with an agenda that is focused on either philosophical or social change—today's American Progressive Movement. This process creates social conflict between those that support the new direction and those that oppose it and push back against the new ideas; even if the stated goal is to enhance the quality of life for individuals. If the change agenda wins, new laws will be passed, new programs and benefits will be created, which will result in newly expanded and acceptable social interactions, changes in lifestyles, or new taxes and regulations. This will produce widespread acceptance by its proponents in the electorate; or rejection by its opponents producing political discontent and strife. A discontent that is relative and personally felt by the voter and viewed as a failure of correct thinking and producing a progressive opposition described by these five step:

- Anger over outcomes, but which become acceptable over time.

- Animosity towards the opposition which deepens over time.
- Hatred and unwilling acceptance of the opposition's victory.
- Self-righteous and emotional judgment in the extreme towards the winning opposition
- Threatened revenge, in whatever form it takes, reflected in both rhetoric and action.

Examples abound of these responses which are wrapped in the philosophies, ideologies, and political issues of the day. Over time disputed and proactive political change causes strife, stifles investment, creativity and productivity, and diminishes the upside potential of the entrepreneur, the source of all productive capital. In the process a new worldview is declared; a process accompanied by emotional acceptance and a decline in knowledge, risk and opportunity.

Some with great political power may view change as necessary and beneficial, enhancing their personal position; but others view this as an overreach which should be rejected. When all of these factors are combined they have a direct impact on the success or failure of a society, reflecting internal conditions, as well as external regional and global ideological realities. Citizens should distrust the overreach and promises (a recommended and major paradigm shift in the existing habits and forms of the nation) made by politicians; all have an unanticipated consequence.

11

PROGRESS

CHASING OPPORTUNITY

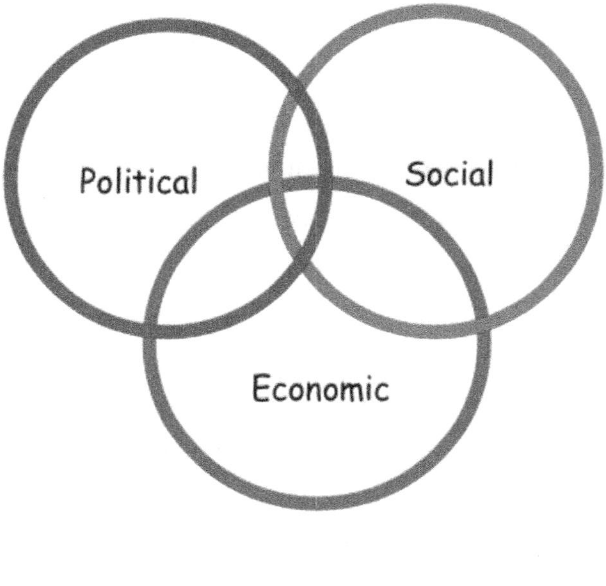

Progress: The gem at the center of the social, economic and political elements.

Previously in 'Balancing the Tensions' the interaction between the social, political and economic environments was described and explaining how the interaction of these elements produces progress. It was further noted that permanent progress can only occur at the intersection of all three elements; each element impacted by the circumstances and opportunities present within it; each in constant motion and reacting to the positive and negative events created by the others. For progress to occur it requires that the structure of the market place—for new ideas and products—is defended by a political structure that supports and protects it.

However, progress itself was not previously described, as progress is often interpreted and applied through the lens of the worldview. For some progress is the overall advancement of society caused by advances in their social and economic conditions. For others, it is purely measured through a paradigm shift in social thinking as promoted by a particular interest group: for example, a court decision which legitimizes a particular social desire. Still, for others it is the use of political power to advance an agenda which produces a favorable, but selective, outcome, or that progress is measured simply through the change in the creation of wealth. Depending on the perspective and the applied use of personal knowledge, experience and expectations, an individual's worldview will be defined by their view of progress. If their view is positive, these perspectives fundamentally change the social and economic fiber of the community resulting in a perceived gain—progress. If the perception is negative then the result is the opposite, a stagnant view of society accompanied by a political promise to change the social and economic conditions through the use of applied power.

Progress is a measurement of the social and economic advancement of a nation's people, supported, not caused, by the structure of government. In any modern society of free people, government serves in response to their needs, not as the instigator of society's progress. Government is not a co-equal partner; but a reflection of the people who created it and their motivated self-interests. An example of where progress wasn't served was the passage in the Southeastern United States of the Jim Crow laws beginning in 1877. Given the circumstance and in the pursuit of opportunity black migration to the northern states began only to find that there too racism existed. Consequently the needs of the Black community weren't served by either national or state political leadership regardless of location. Racism and ignoring the needs of the people effectively created second class citizens across the county. During this time period, progress for blacks and other minorities was inhibited by an entrenched racism that has survived and still exists today in many communities.

A society *cannot* advance without knowledge, risk, competition and equality; these are the essential elements which produce social and economic advancement. If society's world or community view of the marketplace supports equality of opportunity, and if the benefits are shared by all participants, progress will occur. But the economy cannot create change by itself; for society to advance it must also involve the underlying social constructs forming a partnership to create fundamental change and improvement for all participants. There can be no second class citizens.

. . .

Permanent Change

The advancement of free societies is reflected best in the very small area where all three rings of the social, economic and political environments overlap and it is where permanent progress occurs. It is in a free society where its members seek opportunity, pursue knowledge, education and skills development, and benefit from better jobs and higher incomes. The economy responds to this market place condition with investment in innovative new products, in the process it creates more jobs with higher wages producing an expanding market and increased profits. In turn the government supports the expansion of the economy for the tax base that it generates to pay for its programs. For example according to the Wall Street Journal, May 12, 2019, the new 2018 US tax laws increased tax revenues by stimulating private spending and investment. This reflects the impact government can have when it responds to the needs of the people and the economy, not the reverse. If government expands to solve problems through increased taxation and additional regulations when the economy is healthy then progress is squeezed, and the entrepreneurship necessary for the economy to continue to grow and expand is restricted. This is not to argue against taxes and regulation rather that changes should be applied judiciously and only used to advance and protect the needs of the people.

This reflects the very difficult challenges that lie before any modern day republic; the challenge of meeting the needs of individuals, society, and the economy. The process of satisfying these is complicated by the very problems present in each. Individuals, however, always desire to improve and advance their quality of life by seeking new opportunities and higher incomes.

Government follows the process started by individuals through legislative and regulatory means by supporting, or regulating, the means by which individuals apply risk, knowledge and discovery. Regulation intended to protect society and the economy from unscrupulous players and other unknown hazards, environmental and otherwise that transpired in the past. Even with these protections in place America experienced such catastrophes as the chemical dumping by Hooker Chemical into the Love Canal in Buffalo, New York, and the polluting of the Hudson River by General Electric (GE). Both were caused by unregulated chemical dumping in the past and both areas declared hazardous waste sites by the Environmental Protection Agency (EPA). Today Love Canal has been remediated and efforts to clean up the Hudson continue.

To fully understand these interactions, individual attitudes towards the market and political system must be considered. Alternatively, the *order* and structure of the political system must be understood—the application of *justice* provided to the society by the system of governance must be balanced and fair—and, finally, the *freedom* available to choose must be exercised. It is this combination that creates the ability to consume, to innovate, to produce goods, to provide services and to assume risk. The freedom to exploit marketplace opportunities leads to the ultimate creation of social advancement, wealth and personal success.

Risk and Power

When considered in the context of *risk and power*, who has it and who doesn't, who applies it and what outcomes does it produce? The differing roles of the individual and government in regard to these questions clearly define the responsibility each has. Furthermore, the application of their respective principals are brought into the clear as the government holds no risk, but it does hold power. In the absence of governmental risk the ownership of risk is placed squarely on the individual, the citizen, and risk's price is paid directly, and felt through the impact on individual circumstance and economic outcomes.

All societies have some form of order, but the structure of the order depends on its roots and its present day application. Without a system that develops knowledge, protects freedom and encourages risk the individual is laid bare before the power of government. Freedom in all its forms, then, is dependent upon the system of governance and the protections applied through the established judicial system, essential to the protection of the freedom and rights of the individual.

If the order chooses to increase its power then the essential rights of the citizen (the rights of the mind, property, speech and choice) are diminished and the power of the state increases. This power can be applied against any citizen, any time, resulting in the *taking* of individual political freedom and economic independence. This is most often accomplished through taxation and regulation.

If freedom is continuously reduced through the passage of laws, the outcome is the eventual establishment of a progressive socialized, concentrated and/or dictatorial power.

Furthermore, as the state holds no risk vis-a-vis the citizen, the state then holds all power and can apply it at will. And given its unlimited resources the state can easily defend itself against any threat made by its citizens. To defend against the unlimited power of the state, the citizen has little power, great risk, and can lose everything.

. . .

Power, defined and developed in conversation with Paul Cosca, JD, is:

1. The ability to get another to do what you want.

The means to an end; an economic, political or national strategy.

2. There are four forms of power:

(a) Positional: a national leader can use power for good or evil, leadership or control, progress or stagnation

(b) Group identity: has the power to force recognition and change, exerts influence over the media, and has great influence over political leadership

(c) Individual: rooted in knowledge, produces its greatest results when combined with leadership and risk

(d) Market power: the impact of innovation and design

3. Power driven by promises:

(a) The improvement of an individual's quality of life.

(b) They will address social needs to reduce individual burden and risk.

(c) They appeal to the motivated self-interest of the governed.

(d) Offer a better life and greater individual and economic equality.

4. Power requires:

(a) The application of an aligned media (information) with influence exerted over the citizenry. Most effective when couched in a declared righteousness requiring a new paradigm shift.

(b) Acceptance of the *new* agenda

(c) Individual flexibility and willingness to accept and participate in the order's social structure and modified, or reduced, morality. It is the accepted redefinition and expansion of the social good.

(d) A transaction: the acceptance of the order's ideas; entails the willing exchange of individuality and principles for the greater good.

(e) That the opposition be tolerant of the order's demands.

(f) Legal construction: the justification and support for any new direction which justifies additional taxes, regulation, prohibitions and limitations upon the citizen.

5. Those in power will identify, and/or leverage, new internal/external threats to justify its actions.

6. The ultimate threat: the use of force and/or punishment against the governed, innocent citizenry or disaffected interest groups by the government or its appointees.

> *"What really creates discontent in the modern age, as in all ages, is confusion and uncertainty. People turn to radical doctrines not necessarily when they are poor, but when they are emotionally and intellectually distraught. When faith in their world is shaken; when old rulers and old forms of government disappear; when profound economic changes alter their modes of livelihood; when the expectation of private and public change becomes greater than the expectation of private and public continuity; when even the family seems imperiled; when people can no longer live as their ancestors lived before them, but wander bewildered in new ways—then the radical agitator, of one persuasion or another, has a fertile field to cultivate."*
>
> *~Russell Kirk, the American Cause*

California

California is an example of political over-reach, where public policy has overshadowed its intent to serve. The state is in a perennial financial crisis with regionally disparate economies. There exists fast growing high-tech and entertainment centers with high wage pockets in the larger urban areas; these are in sharp contrast to the rural agricultural communities that experience limited economic development and slowly expanding economies.

California also has a rapidly growing population; the US census has estimated that over the past five years California has had over 3.5 percent growth, adding nearly 1.5 million new residents. However, the jobs being created in this expansion have tended to be lower wage service jobs, a fact confirmed by the Institute for Research on Labor and Employment (IRLE) at the University of California, Berkeley. To address this issue Los Angeles is considering a new policy that will mandate a minimum wage of $15.00/hour. L.A.'s policy is an attempt to address, not only the greater problem of low income wage earners, but to reduce or stabilize the ever increasing burden on the city and county's social services.

The problem is more complicated than simply low wages; it is the high cost of Los Angeles living compounded by the surplus of unskilled labor at the lowest income levels. This surplus is created by the failure of the federal government to control immigration at the southern border, on one hand, and the greater economic attractive force of low wage work opportunities in Los Angeles on the other. IRLE's study predicts that an increase in the minimum wage will have a beneficial impact on the standard of living for these low wage earners, but the reality is that providers will also increase their prices to cover the higher labor costs. The study also concluded that raising the minimum wage would add additional costs to the County's regulatory enforcement, the unintended consequence of a policy intended to make the Los Angeles region more affordable.

> *"... (the research) documented the extensive growth of income inequality in California since the late 1970s. The researchers' data showed that California workers at the lowest end of the pay scale have seen significant declines in their earnings over the last three decades, after adjusting for inflation. Workers in the highest income brackets, meanwhile, have seen enormous gains.*
>
> *We are seeing the hollowing out of middle-wage jobs over time according to Annette Bernhardt, a visiting researcher at UC Berkeley's Institute for Research on Labor and Employment. For example, the bottom 20% of workers have seen inflation-adjusted wages decline 12% since 1979, while the top 10% of California workers have seen wages grow 35%. The trend is happening even as low-wage workers as a whole are becoming more educated and have more work experience.*
>
> *About 44% of low-wage workers in California were older than 35 last year, while in 1979 only 32% of workers were that old. Teenagers also make up a much lower share of the low-wage workforce — 5%, compared with 16% in 1979. Nearly half of low-wage workers had at least some college education last year, compared with 39% in the late 1970s."*
>
> *~The LA Times, April 30, 2015, UC Berkeley's IRLE*

Over the past 30 years California's leaders have ignored the varying market opportunities that its climate and economic environment spawned during World War II and during the 1980s manufacturing and high technology booms. However, there are other conditions at play including the impact of existing laws and regulations that have had a negative impact. While it is still the nation's, and the world's, greatest hub for innovation and entertainment, its large industrial and innovative manufacturing base, and associated capital investments are moving to other locations. Companies are reacting to regulations, higher taxes and rising costs, and are making economic decisions that improve their own operating costs in a globally competitive market place. For example, companies leave California for competing lower cost, lower regulation, and lower taxing states. Most recently Toyota moved its US headquarters from Torrance, California, to Plano, Texas; a loss of 4,000 direct jobs and their related wages to the LA area. Higher-wage jobs that will not be easily offset by simply increasing the minimum wage.

Eras that laid the foundations for so many new industries and higher wage and higher order thinking-technical jobs in the Golden State, are now being replaced and exchanged for an ever-expanding local service industry with lower wages.

For California all is not lost, businesses are creating new high-wage jobs driven by knowledge-based software programing, engineering and entertainment that serves global markets; but, the question remains whether these jobs will be sufficient to offset the lower wages of the services, hospitality and healthcare industries?

The other area of job growth in California is public employment, both in local and state government where tax dollars pay for the basic services of safety, education and protection, but also for an ever expanding demand for social assistance as well. The state's greatest advantage is its economic diversity which includes natural resources, agriculture, technology, entertainment, tourism and so on; a diversity which many states would love to have.

However, the very nature of California's government is a prime example of how the *order* has attempted to create a better social and natural environment at the expense of the greater needs of the economy and the advancement of its people.

Today, California is ranked 29 for business climate by Forbes Magazine (Best States for Business, 2018). This compares negatively to neighboring and competing states nationally. North Carolina is ranked number one (1), Utah is ranked number two (2), Texas is ranked number three (3), Colorado is ranked number eight (8), Arizona is ranked number 17 and Nevada and Oregon are ranked number 21 and 22 respectively. The top five states for Job growth in 2018 were Nevada number one, Utah number two, Idaho number three, Arizona number four and Washington number five according to *www.statista.com*. In the *Best States for Business, 2015* issue, job growth projections had Arizona ranked number one, Nevada at number two and Utah at number three. Utah is viewed as the low cost alternative to California for high tech jobs. All states had wages, incomes and cost of living lower than California.

Meanwhile California has continued to grow from population increases and high technology development, but is it creating insufficient high-skilled high-paying new jobs outside the high-tech economic segment? When combined with low-skilled immigration, the state has created fewer and fewer skilled jobs resulting in localized pockets of wealth and spreading, low-income communities.

This has been further compounded by California's recent drought and the declining availability of water for its agricultural sector. California's food production declined by $5 Billion, a ten percent reduction in food production, according to Bloomberg (Elizabeth Campbell and Megan Durisin, Jan 28, 2014), and it has struggled to recover to its former production levels. This has further impacted the number of jobs associated with food production across the state forcing a shift in workers from rural agricultural areas to the urban cities in search of work, once again expanding the low-wage service sector labor market.

California has pursued social and environmental policies in a progressive manner but which, it would seem, gave limited consideration to the cost of either their adoption, impact on the cost to its residents, new regulations, or the competition from other states.

The condition of the state has further been complicated by an incestuous relationship between government employee unions and state legislators. This has further raised the cost of government, increased regulation and the cost to citizens and business. Today, it is more cost effective for manufacturing, high-wage/high-volume jobs, to leave the state and sell to California than to remain and be a part of it. An example of this is Tesla's new $5 Billion battery plant in Reno. The result is a conflicted state with disparate regions of economic growth versus those struggling with, and fighting against, economic stagnation.

Arguably the primary cause for California's declining competitive position can be attributed to Proposition 1A in 1966 which established a year round legislature; this single event contributed to, and increased, the power of special interest groups and public employee unions which contribute to the re-election campaigns of year round salaried legislators. This single event produced the professional California politician paid for by tax payers and re-elected by special interests. Over the past 50 years this single proposition has contributed the most to creating America's largest single party state; no issue, no law too small to get attention.

Secondly, California's Proposition 14, in 2010, was perhaps the nail in California's declining competitive position; it established that the two top vote getters in a single all comers primary would be the two candidates on the state's general election ballot. As a state with a Democrat registration of 60-65 percent, it essentially eliminated any competition of ideas. In its most recent elections the state has had run-offs only between two democrat candidates. All other parties are essentially blocked out. Today, the races are all about who can out-*progressive* the opposing candidate. The state is now the first state to essentially become a single party state. There are several other states that are close, but none that have so effectively eliminated the competition through the plurality vote.

Today the state continues to seek new revenue resources (taxes) to pay for the commitments its politicians and bureaucrats have created, while failing to meet the greater public obligations of a healthy, statewide, dynamic economy. The idea of *to protect and serve* has been lost, replaced by the power of the political class and special interests; each driven by a political philosophy that government has the power, and the special interest has the ideas. Combined these produced a legislative environment driven by regulation and a never-ending list of wants to be satisfied by the unrestricted power of the political class. This has been compounded by the state's ever expanding demand for socialized benefits, all coming at the expense of the economic potential of the state and its communities.

California has failed as a *political* state in which competitive ideas create better solutions to complex problems. This raises the specter of whether or not the state will be able to meet its obligations in the long term if not supported by the Federal government's deficit spending, essential to providing the necessary revenue to sustain the growth and welfare of its society in a nationally and globally competitive environment.

Even with all the challenges created by the state some cities like Santa Barbara, Irvine and Palo Alto remain at the top of the list for quality of life, according to www.Livability.com. However, the cost of living is substantially higher than in other communities within the state. By monitoring this complex system of competitive affordability and politics we can make certain assumptions about California's political structure, its society, economy, status and future; and through it the discovery and implications for other states and communities. Given these conditions, California may well serve as a model for predicting the fate of other states and nations based on the three very simple ideas of order, justice and freedom.

To have real progress a society must apply these essentials in a continuous never ending process, whose end product is a combination of knowledge, competition, risk (physical and monetary) and power.

There are no short cuts or direct paths to progress. An individual, or a society, cannot advance from knowledge to power to purpose and progress without the interim steps of risk and competition. Any attempt to go from knowledge to power fails to produce progress. It cannot be wished for, nor dictated by the passage of legislation. Progress is never achieved if the essentials of the marketplace are ignored or are not present.

Essential to the market in all its forms is truth. Truth becomes a fundamental operating condition, without truth there can be no trust in the veracity between parties, no confidence in product and great suspicion in pricing. In the short-run markets may operate just fine, but in the long term they can grow stagnant or even collapse from within; the Enron experience. To ensure a long-term positive outcome truth is essential, it is represented by the modern day performance contracts which every individual, company and nation enters into, whether contract or treaty. It establishes the transactional norm, and enforces the ethical and expected long-term transactional relationship. Progress relies upon this advancement and leverages the application of truth (ethical behavior, the moral standard, one willing to do for the other) to produce success.

Within this context nations attempt to redefine economics and social relationships through a process which extends socialized benefits and reduces individual risk. However, it must be understood that without risk and competition, progress and social constructs are weakened; any attempt to reduce risk produces a decline in competition and lays the foundation for economic stagnation and increased social tensions.

In Europe the nations of the European Union (EU) are a good example of this through their attempts to reduce personal risk by shifting the tax burden to companies while offering a myriad of socialized benefits deemed as necessary for the public good. In Europe there are nations that are entrepreneurial (Great Britain,

Germany, France for example) and there are those that rely heavily on their neighbors and tourism to survive (Greece, Italy and Spain for example). According to the European Commission Tourism Report, March, 2014, France has 90 million visitors each year contributing nearly 10 percent to its overall GDP. In Italy tourism represented over 13 percent of its GDP for 2017 according to www.statistica.com. Without tourism and its employment and tax contributions European nations would struggle to support all of their governmental programs. A well developed and opportunistic economy produces amazing results and it supports many jobs and collects enormous taxes for the socialized benefits that these nations offer. Tourists, companies and nations trust that transactions will occur as promised. These types of transactions produce an economy built on the pursuit of knowledge and truth and enforced by the contractual agreement. Regardless of the nation, knowledge, risk and truth are the prime movers in every social environment and competitive marketplace in which societies participate.

The Role of Government

If government is to have a role in both the progress of a nation and its stability what is it?

> *"... establishing the principles of Freedom (is) to say that Government is a compact between those who govern and those who are governed; but this cannot be true, because it is putting the effect before the cause; for as man must have existed before governments existed, there necessarily was a time when governments did not exist, and consequently*

there could originally exist no governors to form such a compact with.

The fact therefore must be that the individuals themselves, each in his own personal and sovereign right, entered into a compact with each other to produce a government: and this is the only mode in which governments have a right to arise, and the only principle on which they have a right to exist."

~Thomas Paine, The Rights of Man

A nation's progress is fully dependent upon its system of governance, its structure and actions directly and indirectly influence it. Depending on how government's positive and negative acts are perceived in the social and economic market place opportunity is either captured and advanced or limited. For example, bureaucratic centralized government structures are incapable of reacting quickly to local and national market opportunities given their existing regulations, taxes and policies. Whereas centralized political power restricts access to capital, limited multi-level governments can respond quicker leveraging capital to satisfy the infrastructure needs of their citizens and businesses; capital spending authorized and paid for by its citizens.

The fundamental political and regulatory culture of government is incapable of moving swiftly enough to leverage and support new market opportunities; therefore its best role is to be a regulator. Any attempts to become a market maker will end in failure given entrenched bureaucracies and interests. Just as government can support market opportunity it can also lay the foundation for doing great things or failure through its power to limit capital. For example, in America the Federal Government has supported and maintained the National Park System, it supports the federal highway system, it partners with and supports the maintenance of airports through the Federal Aviation Administration, it dredges navigable rivers through the Army Corps of Engineers, it contributes to the expansion of local water and sewer systems. Good things that support improvements that provide for safe and healthy living.

As politicians are naturally risk averse and intent on preserving power they rely heavily on delivering funding for local projects and on bureaucracies to execute their decisions. However, heavily centralized governments deem it as an essential obligation to provide guidance and control over all economic and social systems; a fete accomplished through the legal, benefit and regulatory process. Regulation and taxation are the means of controlling economic outcomes; social benefit the means of avoiding social upheaval; all are defined and implemented by the institutional structure. In the end, it is ultimately the structure of government that determines the success or failure of the economic landscape and progress.

Progress in the cities.

Government's role is perhaps best reflected in the historic rise and impact in the capital city of many nations. Centralized power, while necessary to the development and definition of a nation is also essential to the execution of its political mandates. Throughout history capital cities have demonstrated this exercise of power and authority over the governed; a power reflected in the subsequent economic growth and power of virtually every capital city around the world: Rome, Paris, London, Beijing, Moscow, Tokyo, Mexico City, and Washington DC. And, through their bureaucracies and offices, this institutionalized power executed their mandates exerting control over their territories, society and the economy.

The rise of economic power, in capital cities, is attributable to two primary forces: first, the seat of all national power; and second, the ability to tax and control the resources of an entire nation. As the center of power, capital cities were the first to benefit from the organization and need for loyal workers and their subsequent expansion into the physical realm through the construction and development of related infrastructure: roads, water, sewer, castles for defense, and palaces for royalty. All these are essential to demonstrating the military and economic power of a nation and region.

During the Industrial Revolution and as a result of this early investment, capital cities were the first to rise; with their centralized power, money and infrastructure they experienced the impact of new and emerging industry. Infrastructure became the means, and essential qualifier, in the development and attraction of new industries and workers, ultimately becoming government's new source of money, creating economic diversity and advancing opportunity.

During the subsequent urbanization era, people worked hard and long hours for little pay, regardless of age or gender; the predictable nature of manufacturing transformed not only cities but also the underlying power of government. Regardless of the conditions the predictable nature of this work was better than trying to eke out a living on a small low production farm, especially given the unpredictable nature of weather.

Contrary to other historical capitals, America as a union of independent states, had a decentralized government; local governments made critical infrastructure decisions and were given the taxing authority to pay for it, an essential component for the development of a diverse economy and the creation of economic growth hubs. In the past American cities developed around resources, infrastructure and innovation, such as with Detroit's auto industry, Pittsburgh's production of steel, New York's financial centers; Houston's oil refining, and Chicago for its railroads. Today, the San Francisco Bay Area, and Seattle, support the development of global high tech companies. These centers created high wage specialized employment, and attracted the requisite middle income workers.

This has become part of the shared experience in large cities where employment is supported by diverse industries; everything from food production to manufacturing, aerospace, software and other high tech industry fields; financial, and health services. This is all supported by expansive infrastructure including: low to high cost housing alternatives, commercial real estate in all its forms, and diverse educational resources with a high degree of career variability and choice. In the process both institutional and economic power is advanced.

Large cities offer an abundance of choice in jobs for people of talent, and for those who are skilled and unskilled seeking opportunity. However, in some employment markets, little has changed. Today it is no longer the hiring of high numbers of workers for manufacturing, but rather the hiring of large numbers of workers with low skills, laboring in common competitive retail and health services. For the low-skilled not much has changed from the long hours of the industrial revolution, with little pay for the unskilled work experience.

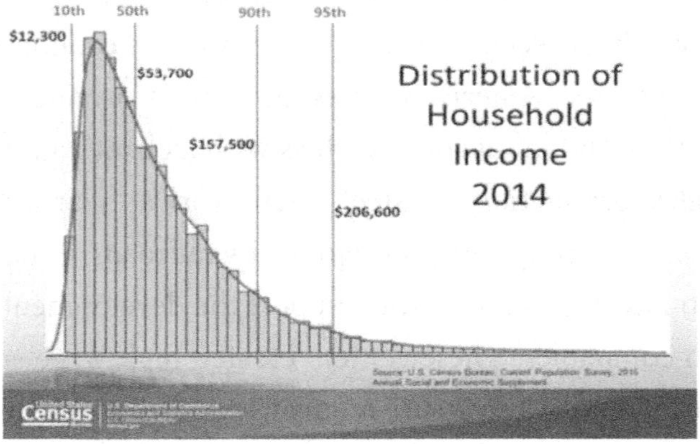

Large cities create and advance the social politic of a region, state or nation through local efforts which seek solutions to real and perceived social and economic barriers. In large cities the illusion of progress is ever present, reflected in the steady drumbeat of community leader statements which, in today's marketplace of ideas, is re-enforced by an ever present mass media and the applied use of personal social media, twitter and Facebook for example. While opportunity may be created in the large city it is also accompanied by the dominant and accepted group think; for the individual and unless backed by money they are lost in this *milieu*.

Given the complexity of economics and the power of urban politics, small cities, regardless of location, are simply unable to compete against these large economic and social movers. By extension, small cities are influenced by these culture shifts and major social trends created by a mass media in all its forms; meanwhile, these communities struggle to preserve their foundational and historic character and way of life. These communities, while living in the shadows of big cities, are affected evermore by national and global economic events and political forces. However, for these communities, progress remains dependent upon their locals economic circumstances, but also dependent upon the acceptance of the greater society's advancements.

Historically, small cities rely upon the power of local leaders, cultures and unique lifestyles to preserve their quality of life. Small cities have less social complexity, a lower cost of living, a stronger sense of community; in small cities all problems are known and shared; and a recognition by the young that to succeed one must leave home to find opportunity. Today, in small communities financial success is difficult to come by as they remain dependent upon external money for meeting the daily demands of their lives and businesses.

Is Progress then a function of growth and size?

The answer to this question is a very definite 'no.' For large and small cities the demand for assistance is unrelenting, the driver in each instance is the perennial demand for economic, social and infrastructure improvements. But when economic progress slows as a result of declining entrepreneurship, investment or national recession, cities are overwhelmed, unable to effectively respond to internal and external forces. They experience a decline in individual income and community resources and an increase in the demands of the underprivileged and destitute. Situations and conditions are made worse by added immigration, as people relocate and seek new opportunity and the need to survive. In communities with rapid population growth, limited advanced education opportunities, and unfulfilled community economic development, people, given these circumstances, see their efforts dwindle along with their aspirations.

In the short term, the primary driver in any market is whether or not individuals accept (consume) or reject the goods and services produced by the market; and, whether or not they evolve socially and economically to effect the necessary change that produces progress. In this mix, government's role is to enable the individual, and by extension, society, to determine their present and future circumstance. In response, individuals react to policy decisions by asking the question: Do these policies serve the advancement of personal knowledge, risk and competition in addressing the present and future needs of the community? Society will determine the above by accepting, tolerating or rejecting these policies through their individual pursuits, application of knowledge, judgement of circumstance and voting.

As a result, progress itself can be hindered depending upon how communities prioritize issues, define the problem, and create solutions. For example, when a community fails to identify the root causes of a problem, it forces the community to focus on the issue by solely considering its present plight.

Communities exist in the context of their location, historical economic fundamentals and public policies. Caught between these forces communities struggle to change the decisions of the past to advance the present. Consider Phoenix and Tucson, Arizona, two cities separated by less than 120 miles. Metropolitan Phoenix, as the state capital, has the additional advantage of being centrally located in the state, has competing utilities giving customers choice, and an ample, though over-subscribed, water supply through the Salt River Project and Central Arizona Project. In addition, there are 24 competing municipalities in the metropolitan area, each competing with the others for development and economic power. Urban growth has been one of the hallmarks of this competition with each city defining its boundaries and economic niche as part of the larger metropolitan area. For example, Chandler, a Phoenix suburb, is dominated by high tech industry and high wages, the product of the silicon desert; Sun City, retirement and services; Scottsdale, tourism and quality of life; Glendale, sports; Phoenix, government, manufacturing, distribution, services and transportation (Sky Harbor Airport); and Tempe, Arizona State University and retail services. Every city has defined itself and works to retain and enhance its position vis a vis the competition.

Tucson has seven cities in its urban shadow, many of which have been incorporated within the past 20 years, and with much smaller populations. Furthermore, Tucson's geography and land use has resulted in 36 percent of its population living in unincorporated areas; as a result, county policies are less focused on the competition between cities, but instead are driven by policies that preserve the rural nature and low density residential housing which dominates the non-metro areas. As a consequence, the expansion of infrastructure and the solving of problems are complicated given the politics and the related costs of expansion. Today many would say that Tucson has a better quality of life even though its economy is less robust.

Given these differences the following table highlights some of the critical economic conditions which, in the end, complicate the competitive nature of the cities.

US Census Bureau (est. 2016)	City of Phoenix	City of Tucson
Population	1,615,017	530,706
Population Metro Area	4,490,000	1,010,025
Median Housing Price (Zillow)	227,300	174,700
Education High School	80.9	84.4
Education Bachelors	27.4	25.8
Median Income	$49,328	$37,973
Foreign Born	15.2%	19.8%
Manufacturing Shipments ($1,000)	$12,978,949	$1,551,529

*US Census Data (2015 estimates)

In studying the table two major differences appear. First, there is the difference in median incomes for the two cities; second, there is the difference in manufacturing shipments. One can conclude that it's not the difference in education levels, but rather the location, population size, and infrastructure advantages, which enable Phoenix to dominate the Arizona market place. This is complimented by its two hour proximity advantage to California, and the near-hub advantage of Phoenix's Sky Harbor Airport.

Tucson struggles to compete economically given reduced income levels and the subsequent lesser disposable income; economically, Tucson lags behind the Phoenix metro area. This is reflected in the poverty rate of both metro areas: Phoenix 16.2 percent, and Tucson, 18.9 percent. Arguably, Tucson's biggest promotional advantage is its quality of life, and the research capabilities of the University of Arizona.

Every community, city and state across the nation, and around the world, struggle to solve many of the same social and economic issues. There are cities that are more successful than others given leadership and prior economic conditions, and opportunities which produce diverse lifestyles and choices offered to, and acted upon, by the resident and business.

Depending upon the power of the motivating forces, local issues will either be addressed by the broader community or ignored and abandoned over time. Regardless all issues produce a shared experience which citizens will debate internally and across neighborhoods.

When individuals accept their present circumstance and recognize that present conditions limit opportunities, it is only at that point that moderate progress can occur as expectations demand that alternate choices be made. Business and policy leaders will re-think the present and seek solutions which may come from unexpected sources. For example, if a primary source of employment experiences a serious decline and major layoffs ensue—Boeing Aircraft's layoff of 50,000 employees in Seattle in the early 1970s as an example—then individuals will make alternative choices. Seattle's economic decline was so severe that a billboard was made asking for the last resident leaving to turn out the lights.

However, new industries were born in Seattle that transformed the city such as Microsoft, Starbucks, Amazon, Real Networks, and many other companies such as these laid the foundations for its rebirth.

Under recessionary conditions government policies will be viewed either positively or negatively, attempts are made to support progress and find solutions to desperate problems. If change is preferred, and the status quo rejected, then people will pursue change through the modification of government's direction with a mix of new leadership, which promises to addresses its concerns and advance opportunity. Most recently, the 2016 American presidential election showed the citizens of more states viewed the direction of the prior eight years as a negative and its present direction restricting opportunity. The election reflected the demand for a change.

Citizens will determine the degree to which change is advanced when the existing power structure is either supported, staying the course, or refuted and new expectations declared. Under most circumstances voters will approve the middle ground, rejecting some leaders and approving others, rejecting and approving some voter and policy initiatives, all done with an eye on social policies and costs. If change is desired it creates an alternative paradigm which advances the necessary conditions for progress. In the extreme, if the status quo is rejected all together and change is demanded in its strongest terms, revolutionary change will come with the caveat that the future remains unknown but it is preferable to the present. Leadership will again play a role and depending on how the new structures are seen; the citizens alone will determine the conditions for the future.

> *"Prudence, indeed, will dictate that governments long established should not be changed for light and transient causes; and accordingly all experience hath shown that mankind are more disposed to suffer, while evils are sufferable than to right themselves by abolishing the forms to which they are accustomed."*
>
> *~Thomas Jefferson, the Declaration of Independence*

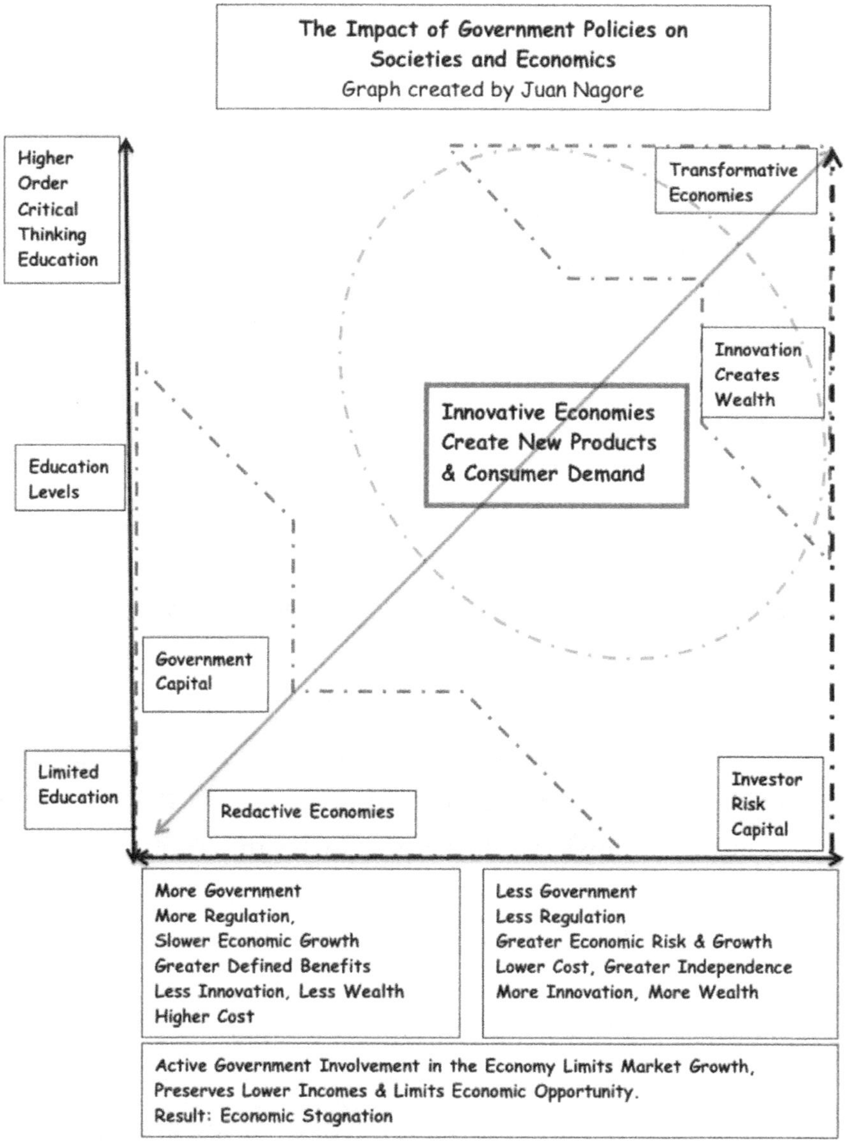
The Impact of Government Policies on
Societies and Economics
Graph created by Juan Nagore
Higher Order Critical Thinking Education
Education Levels
Limited Education
Transformative Economies
Innovation Creates Wealth
Innovative Economies Create New Products & Consumer Demand
Government Capital
Redactive Economies
Investor Risk Capital
More Government
More Regulation,
Slower Economic Growth
Greater Defined Benefits
Less Innovation, Less Wealth
Higher Cost
Less Government
Less Regulation
Greater Economic Risk & Growth
Lower Cost, Greater Independence
More Innovation, More Wealth
Active Government Involvement in the Economy Limits Market Growth,
Preserves Lower Incomes & Limits Economic Opportunity.
Result: Economic Stagnation

12

THE POLITICAL APPLICATION

INJUSTICE CREATES OPPRESSION

The essence of justice is to be the arbiter of disputes, regardless of cause. An outcome is judged as prescribed by the existing standard established in the law and its precedents. In both criminal and civil cases the lawful and unlawful acts of citizens are judged according to the system in place. Justice is further called upon to be the arbiter in issues regarding the use, and abuse, of power by the state. In many instances the judicial system is fair, but given the human factors associated with judicial rules, evidence, procedures and juries, the outcome may not be what was originally desired.

In others instances, and nations, justice is a function of the hierarchical power supported by the actions of corrupt officials in which fairness and truth may not be a consideration. For example, the summary trials that occurred in Argentina resulted in approximately 30,000 people disappearing between 1976 and 1983, this, according to The International Commission on Missing Persons. Without Constitutional guarantees, and judicial protection, the individual is exposed against the state's judicial, economic and political power. For the citizen risk and power must be recognized, analyzed and their impacts understood. Under the above referenced conditions, the citizen has but one set of tools against the state which include individually held knowledge, and the ability to organize with other like-minded citizens to oppose the economic and political power of the state.

In America, the Fourth and Fifth Amendments to the Constitution, stipulate the procedures which are essential to protecting the rights of the accused; and, which are intended to ensure a fair outcome. These processes are essential to protect the citizen or when the citizen challenges the regulatory power of the state.

If Government is charged with protecting the "general welfare" of the nation can it redefine its power responsibly?

The federal government, in response to the people's desires, works to provide the programs and benefits that we demand, and which politically, they agreed to support and sustain; these include: protection for the environment and the border, national defense, expanding and improving the highway system, protecting travelers, improving our cities, health and scientific research, providing healthcare, providing education, providing loan guarantees to businesses, students and homeowners, ensuring ample and safe food, etc. According to the US Catalogue of Federal Domestic Assistance the government funds, and provides, over 1,600 different programs that support individuals, institutions, state programs, infrastructure, business and local initiatives. These programs incur future obligations, and someone in the future will have to pay for them; in the process today's politician is protected, appreciated and granted more time in office.

The government has offered these programs, and historically the citizen has not objected to, assuming the burden of risk for their payment, which today has a *payment due* statement on it.

In America, the growth and expansion of political power is achieved through the promise, creation and extension of new benefits and entitlements delivered through new and expanded bureaucracies. The greater the number of social needs identified by interest groups and politicians the greater the possibility of public benefit for citizens. Citizens perceive the solution as an answer to previously unresolved problems; identifying the problem as an existential need in search of resolution. By accepting the solution an *exchange* is effectively created between the citizen and the government.

This exchange grants more power to, and affirms the need for, government intervention. When a benefit is created and granted, and if perceived by the citizen as having little or no cost to the tax payer, there is no reason to object to its provision. As government increases its list of public benefits its power and influence expands; meanwhile the economic independence and power of the individual, and the market economy, decreases.

The state has the ability to create and influence public opinion and perception through its power to introduce issues and to offer government sponsored solutions. While this may be necessary it may lead to further intrusion into the lives of citizens. Through this process it supports its own political objectives; with power any need, any action can be justified.

The idea that Americans will pursue their own happiness, has the potential to become a declining dream, one converted to shared obligation and perhaps, at some point, even a permanent loss of opportunity caused by taxes, regulations and the burden of government overhead. If this continues, then who has the obligation to pay for the expanded future cost of the promised benefits? Is it the idea that we can tax ourselves, or some segment of the population (however defined); or, is there truly no limit to what the citizen can be obligated to pay for? If so, there is no limit to whom or how much we can tax, what is the cost to our economic freedom? In the end we all have wants, but we must be prepared to pay for the privileges.

America is at a crossroads; we are the greatest borrower in the history of the world, exceeding $22 trillion and increasing by $1 trillion per year; a burden laid upon the owners of America; its citizens and residents regardless of age or status. The present burden is measured in debt, the potential loss of future market opportunity and certainly future higher taxes, unless objected to by the citizen; higher taxes will be required to pay for programs and benefits subscribed to by the public. Government mandated entitlement programs now approach 65 percent of federal annual spending, or two-thirds of an annual $3.5 to $4 trillion budget, with an annual borrowing need of approximately 12 percent to 15 percent of total spending. It must be noted that this debt exists at the national level and excludes all other state and local debt. This additional debt is estimated at nearly an additional $2 trillion dollars according to Christopher Chantrill (www.usgovernmentdebt.us).

I think the question is not: "Are the government's actions proper and correct to protect the public good?" but rather: "Is it doing its best to ensure the long term economic viability of all Americans regardless of age?" Is the government being judicious in its use of the tax payer's dollars? Does it have an effective system of checks and audits? Is it operating at its highest efficiency, or is it susceptible to fraud and abuse? Is there an effort to protect the citizen's future, or does the citizen inherit the cost-risk in exchange for a failure of political leadership and management? Are the *box checkers* in charge? In either case the citizen remains at risk of political decisions intended to preserve power in exchange for the politically deemed necessities of a modern nation. Or, have we reached the point, as John Adams described in his *Defense of Property,* that the more we accommodate the wishes of special interests and the powerful, we begin to lose the very individual freedom we proclaim to defend? It is the fulfillment of a politically declared desire to serve camouflaged in the creation of solution and benefit.

13

DECISIONS

PRIORITIES, IDEAS, AND COMPETITION

Each of us struggle with the needs of the day; the desires of the heart and the pursuits of life. How blissful it would be to be cared for in the manner of our choosing, to exist in the absence of rushed and compelling demands. We cannot escape the priorities of life at the expense of the ideas and beliefs we conjure, and hold dear, nor can we escape the marketplace in which we live, constrained or unconstrained. Life, and all its intrigues, forces each of us to recognize this competition and to respond through our individual Manview, that requires integrated and evaluative thinking.

To be more capable of responding, and to better understand the forces at play within every individual, and every free and open society, we apply our own internal dialogue available to each of us, and considered within the context of life's circumstances. To explain this more fully, there are four thinking modes present in all individuals, and all decisions are considered in the evaluative and the priority assigned to each. These thinking modes, and their related variables/criteria are: (1) Life's condition, (2) Internal influences, (3) Risk and (4) External influences. Combined they represent 15 variables. However, these four modes do not stand in isolation; rather they represent competing forces present in every individual's thought processes.

To think, to respond, to create, and to have any possibility of success, each variable must be aligned, and combined, with other elements within the four different modes to produce desired decision making outcomes. These four modes and the 15 variables produce critical thinking, and decision making, to every-day problems, creating solutions in response to external factors and situations. Combined these four modes form our synthesized and fully integrated thinking. The 15 variables are:

Life's Circumstance and Condition

1. The extent of political freedom.
2. Our present circumstance in which we live.
3. The impact and extent of personal disabilities.
4. Cost: the satisfaction of individual needs.
5. Cost: the satisfaction of individual wants.

Internal Thought

1. Knowledge: the application of education, discovery, opportunity and risk.
2. Philosophy: the learning and application of life principles.
3. Faith: understanding of love and trust
4. Morals: the idea of doing more for the other person than yourself, causing no harm.

. . .

Risk

1. Risk, the critical decision variable; impacts health, well-being and finances.

External Influence

1. Information: what the individual subscribes to, and its interpretation and application.
2. Environmentalism.
3. Gender Issues: how it is identified and applied by the individual.
4. Race Issues: how individuals apply, and recognize, the rights of others, positive and negative.
5. Income Inequality: what I've earned vs what I deserve.

The following depiction combines the four modes and variables, in a graphic image, reflecting the alignment of the competing forces that produce our associated and integrated decision making:

Internal Dialogue

Decision Modes and Variables

Created by Juan Nagore

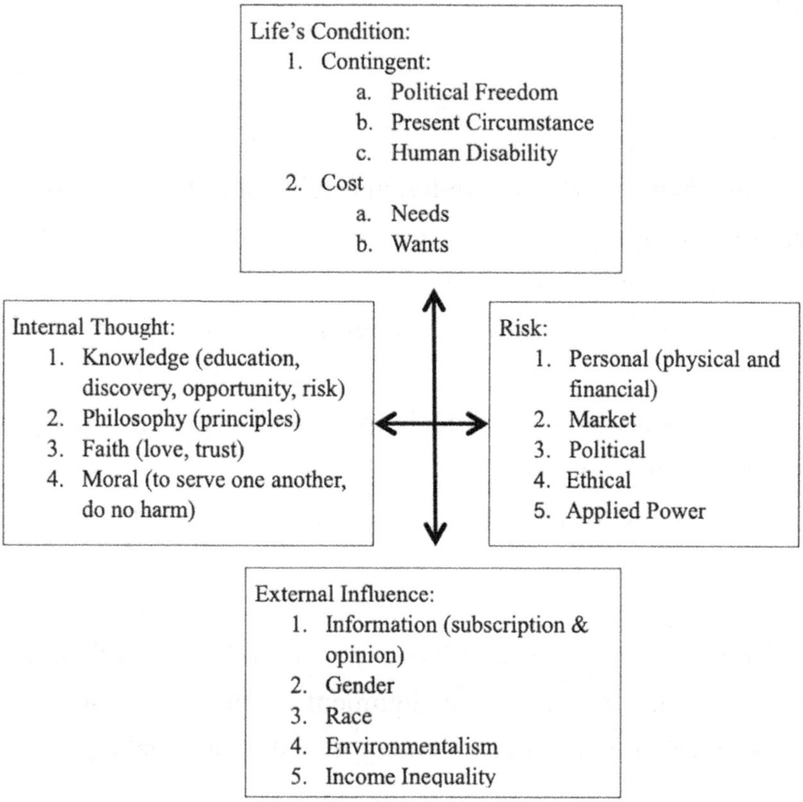

> Complete thinking requires the integration of the various decision making criteria and consideration of the applicable variables.

As a structured entity, these variables appear as competing interests. In actuality these represent the whole of the informed individual pursuing an internal dialogue, which encompasses the whole of the person using the fullest application of their knowledge and beliefs. This analysis influences, and determines, choice throughout the individual's social network and decision making process. Depending on the seriousness of the issue at hand, and the more thoughtful the individual is, the more variables get incorporated into the evaluative process, creating an internal discussion that leads to clarity of risk, position, purpose and action. (OODA Theory: Observe, Orientate, Decide, and Act, Colonel John Boyd, US Air Force) A person can reach out for input, but the decision remains his and hers alone.

The first mode, life's condition, represents those circumstances which define the outward existence of our individual life. These are the outward conditions of our lives, where we live, what we encounter, and determine how we survive and prosper; these are the overarching conditions that define the "what, where, and opportunities" of life. These are also the foundation for determining risk. Effectively all decision making is based on these conditions determining life's priorities and opportunities, and are the ultimate, qualifying factors present in every decision.

Political freedom is the number one condition which lays the foundation for all other modes. In a free society we trust the government to be responsible for providing a healthy supportive environment; the ability to live life free of disability if possible or to provide the means to offset its punishments. And, to further ensure the economic market place to satisfy life's needs and wants. Absent these the individual is limited in what he or she can accomplish in the pursuit of life's happiness.

The second mode, internal thought; these variables represent individual attributes which constitute individual knowledge, deliberate thought, and evaluative context and beliefs. Decision making influenced by knowledge, philosophy, faith and morals, creates an independence which is less affected by external factors, and which permits us to evaluate risk in the broader context of life. These factors are not prescribed through the dictate of obedience but by choice, it is the product and application of our knowledge. Issues, conflicts, ideas, and social movements are all evaluated and judged against these principles, and not the social context of one's life which has alternative demands. In the application of internal thinking, ideas and choices are questioned and analyzed leading to effective action, it is the application of Boyd's "Observe, Orientate, Decide and Act" theory. When individuals practice knowledge and experience, and then apply philosophy and faith, their search for solutions is more likely to produce effective and productive outcomes. Internal thinking demands that questions be asked in the pursuit of the most effective response and solution.

Risk, the third mode, is not a factor in every decision, but is often the variable which should be considered in all critical decisions affecting personal matters, or when personal or financial well-being is a factor. When considering risk other factors are easily eliminated with the decision focused solely on the critical aspects of personal harm or financial cost. Under these circumstances no effective or critical decision can be made quickly without including it in the final analysis. For the best outcomes risk must be part of any consideration in order to obtain the most satisfying outcomes and solutions.

Finally, external influences represent the social movements which individuals consider critical to the definition of their quality of life. These movements are evaluated subject to the priority assigned to each by the individual self-defined social construct and outward associations. We give these movements voice and adopt them as part of our social views and interactions. These movements reflect our broadest views about information, gender, race and income inequality; and, reflect our present thinking, paradigms and chosen associations. We accept these as matter of reality and subscribe to, and listen to, its voice. Decision making, focused on external factors, reflect our interpretation of the critical nature of social issues within our greater community. We accept it for what it is; complex issues evaluated on the basis of its importance in our belief hierarchy. Each issue may be perceived as a crisis created by the inability of the individual to overcome circumstance, or the failure of society to address and solve the conditions at the center of the problem. Through its broad appeal, a crisis can take on a life of its own, supported by leadership and the media, voices which can influence and dominate the culture.

The nine variables represented by the internal and external criteria, establish our views of the world. These driving forces shape our worldview and our Manview. For internal thought to be effective trust is necessary in our knowledge, ethical behavior and the positive acts of others. The four internal variables all lead to this implicit outcome; to not only be moral, but to trust that another will be equally so. For external thought, awareness of the world is the essential element, which follows from the importance attributed to each of the variables. Each of the five variables produces its own priority which in turn develops and advances its own secular agenda.

These four modes are juxtaposed in our internal dialogue and issues evaluated based upon their relative importance to each of us. These influence our priorities, define our ultimate temporal or spiritual views of the world, and are influenced by our interpretation of the power and righteousness of associations, group think, events, media, and leadership.

Given the urgency of any crisis, a movement is born with great appeal to our external thinking. We perceive this wrong as a product of our lesser selves, or a failure of society, problems which could have been solved if only there had been sufficient forward-thinking and consideration. These issues are based on the perceived need to develop a greater social good by solving a particular problem created by the perceived failure of society. Or, the failure of our government to act when it could have protected a particular group or natural environment. Or, a court decision which would have permitted a particular behavior. These issues are often raised by single individuals or a movement committed to the correction or advancement of a righteous cause. This view is present in, and evaluated in, the context of our self-defined social justice, the combination of our prioritized internal and external thinking, with the idea that its pursuit will produce the greatest good, in the broadest context, for the greatest number of people.

Regardless of the issue, these causes are supported with great emotion requiring immediate action and urgent relief; demanding that the issue be addressed at the highest levels of political and legal decision makers. Furthermore, it requires recognition, if not the acceptance, of the issue at hand, while seeking a solution to the problem at the highest levels. This begs the question: Without a comprehensive analysis and understanding of the complexity of an issue, can effective solutions be found when the cries for solutions demand immediate action? For example, illegal immigration; many see it as the right of an individual to live wherever he chooses without condition, while others will argue that the standard of law must be uniformly applied. The former will have the loudest voice; regardless, the law must be recognized as the greater will of the people. Therein lays the conflict; creating an effective solution to a problem which is politically and emotionally complex while paradoxically challenging ideological differences, in order to arrive at a satisfactory moral, political and legal answer.

Is it Progress or is it Division?

All communities struggle to one degree or another. For example, how does a community improve and deliver upon a state-of-the-art fair, educational system? This battle for better education follows the desire for safe communities, both of which are essential to advancing progress. Historically, to expand and improve an education system has been challenging given the problems of location, incomes, language, revenue and expense. Which leads to the question of who pays and how much? Equality of education is but one example of the demands that exist in communities, and which can exacerbate community conflict by producing differentiated outcomes, and not what was originally intended. In this scenario the politicians are expected to address, and solve, issues founded on the premise that progress requires new solutions to be advanced and implemented. By failing to effectively analyze the cause(s) of the problem, the process itself automatically limits the solutions available.

It is through the combination of individuals supporting causes that society determines its priorities; and, through the process defines its preferences and its social and political alignments. Whether alone or in a group, movements initiated with great emotion take on a life of their own, and must have mass appeal to mobilize action.

Social movements led by individuals who have identified great wrongs, must develop an urgency about their issues which must be resolved politically. To this extent there are many examples of individuals who have put their ideas into play, that span the scope of movements over the past two centuries: John Muir with the environment; Karl Marx with communism; Margaret Sanger with Eugenics and Planned Parenthood; Cesar Chavez with the National Farm Workers Association; Alicia Garza with Black Lives Matter; The Vietnam Anti War Movement, and so on.

When community issues are raised by social movements they create new tensions by demanding change of those in power. As independent calls to address these singular issues arise, there is an accompanying political demand which requires that new alliances be formed. Furthermore, along with community support, new causes require mobilizing the media to amplify awareness in order to motivate political alliances in a direction that leverages existing power structures. Without political support these issues will not receive the necessary advocacy or publicity for long term survival. An example of a political alliance that has been extraordinarily effective is the LGBTQ movement in San Francisco; an effective application and transformation of society through the alliance and power of politicians, media and special interest.

At the onset of any new issue, power is shared between the powerful and the weak; gradually power is taken by the powerful causing a decline in the recognition of the originators; power owned, power shared and power lost. Success or failure depends on the perceived political advantage of each cause by those that would leverage it for political gain. Regardless of the demand for change, the same factors are present in the competition between an individual's internal and external thinking; factors which are influenced by the effectiveness of the message, and the willingness to accept or reject the idea out of hand, after evaluating and considering the righteousness of the issue.

What does this have to do with progress?

At the very heart of progress is knowledge. It reflects the effectiveness of the education system and life experiences; effective education generates discovery which creates opportunity, and produces a willingness to pursue risk. When knowledge is combined with other internal criteria (philosophy, faith and morals), it produces the motivation to address social wrongs and advance the community. It also reflects the idea that just because a condition exists it does not mean that the solution offered is needed, or that it must be addressed through political action. This process produces an internal evaluation of every issue, its related risk and a chosen direction for action.

However, if people think and act solely in their life condition mode, they live in a world dominated by todays needs the only consideration is to survive life's present circumstance. There will always be those limited by ability, the poor and destitute, and their condition must be appreciated, understood and assistance rendered when appropriate by either us or our institutions. Under these conditions future opportunity is extraordinarily limited; knowledge may be constrained by the inaccessibility of education, or the predominant tribal rules of society or the prejudices of the culture itself. Individual pursuits may be aspirational, but the ability to achieve them is out of reach; the individual remains bereft of knowledge and the opportunities the world has to offer.

. . .

What are the consequences?

In a free and open society when issues are raised, whether the thinking is focused on the center, right or left, all are essential components of our integrated decision making. Progress occurs only when individuals and communities apply educated and informed decisions to these criteria for the betterment of all. When everyone considers the multiple cost and benefits to themselves and society, new directions will be either accepted or rejected. Or, as is the case with so many nations, the ability to balance the forces is deferred in favor of the decision making power of the state; under these conditions progress slows then retreats and the advancement of the community is lost over time.

PART IV

THE FUNDAMENTALS

ESSENTIAL 4: THE CONSTANT PURSUIT

14

PURSUIT OF EXCELLENCE

KNOWLEDGE IS TRUTH AND UNDERSTANDING.

As one attempts to define the question of worldview, another factor must be considered in attempting to clarify its definition. To explain this, knowledge, philosophy and truth are applied to the social issues of the day, their relevance to social change, and their impact, acceptance and morality. It is within this context that a person gains an appreciation for another's personal opinion, which is considered in the context of both the question and the response. All social issues are questions that are posited to either satisfy a want or are advanced for the purposes of justifying social change. Today's questions tend to deal with the acceptance of lifestyle choice or life itself at their core, examples include capital punishment versus a life sentence, the drug crisis in all its forms and legalization, the secular freedom from religion versus freedom of religion.

The question and its interpretation is complicated by the perspective and intent of the inquisitor, versus the respondent's clarity of understanding, interpretation, and perspective of the question; all are internalized, evaluated and answered subject to individualized experience and their personal philosophy. The response will vary based upon, background, faith, education, and culture. As such, the question raises the issue, but knowledge becomes the means to communicate and interpret the answer; without clear communication worldview, common ground, Manview, risk, power, social acceptance and morality cannot be clearly understood or expressed.

Given this reality, a new set of ideas is put forth, representing a different set of outcomes. This concept builds on the Internal Dialogue Modes linked to decision making as discussed in the prior section and introduces a morals and social behaviors discussion and their impact on the development of the self, and the extended impact on society. This concept requires the combination of freedom of choice and expression of knowledge to be the foundation for the advancement of society. This fundamental freedom relies upon the choices an individual makes in their interaction with other members of society, a foundation which is either supported by accepted social and moral behavior, or rejected for the same reasons.

As previously stated knowledge is communication, and if progress is to occur the social and political system must concur and support the free expression of choice and its related pursuits. This is America's challenge as the proponents of major issues are divided between left and right as they try to answer the question of who is responsible for whatever obligations are created. Today we argue for an increase in the minimum wage, we question the reasons for the income divide, we ask why are student loans necessary, and how the basic right or need for healthcare should be provided. These are at the top of our must discuss list but not necessarily at the top of our must provide list. Unless compromise is achieved the chaos of division and competing interests will rule the day. To resolve these issues one must have knowledge to see the other side, to understand its consequences, and to seek a satisfactory resolution. However, resolution on complicated issues cannot be achieved in a highly partisan environment in which political objectives restrict the motivation to find solutions. In this entrenched and divided social and political environment how does a single individual expand their understanding of the problem, or define their purpose in its resolution?

This discussion then begins with man's ability to understand ourselves, and to give context, a brief history of knowledge is advanced. Knowledge began with self-awareness of man's individualized understanding of his circumstance and surroundings. Once self-awareness became part of the human experience, man was able to apply first-hand knowledge and experience to the present circumstance. This experience created individual knowledge alerting man to both danger and opportunity. Over the millennia, language and communication followed, and the ability to communicate danger and opportunity could be shared, creating second-hand information, and advancing the shared common knowledge experience. Information became invaluable to supporting the growth and safety of people, tribes and societies. As communication expanded, writing was invented, and history, ideas and inventions, philosophy and faith, could be recorded, shared and understood. From this awareness man developed the ability to identify, and satisfy, his individual needs and wants.

The written word evolved and was spread through religions and education; and, with education, knowledge was systematized and applied. The sharing of knowledge was compressed, accelerated and adjusted for circumstance, advancing the idea of surprise.

> “ ***Surprise Defined:***
> *A discovery (a significant advance)*
> *The application / processing of discovery*
> *Knowledge based (a new science or evolutionary technology)*
> *Opportunity based (market / profit driven)*
> *~George Gilder, "Knowledge and Power"*

Knowledge was applied to answer critical questions, creating discoveries that would satisfy life's needed essentials as defined by circumstance and opportunity, problems were analyzed, and solutions discovered, developed, and applied. Education became the means to share greater and ever evolving information; expanding scientific discovery and creating deeper knowledge. This would then lead to new discoveries, and, when applied in new ways, these would push forward the frontiers of technology. This reasoned contemplation of problems and circumstance resulted in the expansion of applied knowledge; and, of advancing man and societies around the world. The result is an advanced knowledge, new technologies, new industries, reduced poverty and the creation of added opportunity.

This advancement has not been without its trials; the application of knowledge has always been in direct conflict with the competing force of institutional power. This power is the method by which governments support, regulate, control or suppress the advancement of the person. Governments that support knowledge and freedom advance the most. However, those with consolidated power and in the extreme, have used their power to achieve their political objective of domination; often, using fear and corrupt means. They have used this ability to control groups and societies to restrict citizens and deprive them of personal freedom, and to impose the political will of their leaders. The application of power became the means to an end. The most recent example of this is the Maduro dictatorship in Venezuela, which has citizens fleeing in search of food and opportunity.

Man's Pursuit

Within this mix of political and social processes individuals develop their moral and social perspectives, a process complicated by, and reflective of the community's common knowledge, culture and politics. If the institutional power in place chooses to implement its own unique set of standards, it can engender fear and hatred in individuals, groups, religions, nationalities, and races within the greater society. A power structure that supports or pursues a particular agenda, in the short term, will ultimately fail as individuals pursue new opportunity and realities. As such, if there must be a starting point for the application and defense of liberty, it must begin with idea of individual property, both intellectual and real and the natural rights of every person.

Institutional Power, and its methods of applied control and fear, has not changed much over time. But power has been modified and applied over the past century with a softer touch by creating an exchange; a promised, if not delivered, future benefit for power. As a result, a real conflict has existed in virtually every society between those who hold power, and the individually informed, and knowledgeable, citizen on whom society relies upon to function and advance. Today's exchange says "believe in me, vote for me, and I will improve your life." And in some instances, if the vote goes against the power structure by manipulating the outcomes at the ballot box, a leader can achieve the same victory. The tension between institutionalized power and individual knowledge has been, and is, the world's greatest historical conflict.

With this ever present conflict it is amazing that mankind has advanced. Individually held knowledge and applied understanding have repeatedly overcome attempts, by the political class, to render knowledge and intellectual capital the weaker power. To advance the political cause, the powerful have relied upon either the ignorance of the masses playing off unjustified beliefs, opinions, emotion and fear; or by leveraging the promise of benefits and safety for political gain. Facts can be easily dismissed by the powerful through organized communication strategies; limiting facts, segmenting populations, advancing agendas, creating internal and external enemies, creating fear, and blaming the lack of progress on the unenlightened opposition. The powerful seek justification for their actions through the concurrence of the inexperienced, uneducated and powerless; enforced by the disregard for their humanity or rights.

A predictable outcome can then be reached when one considers the absence of an educated, comprehensive analysis by citizens. This exchange most often occurs at the bottom of the hierarchy where economic survival and social agendas coincide; where the need is most prevalent, and economic needs the greatest. The political play is to market the agenda's ideas and political ideologies to the greatest number of people; playing to the needs and emotions of the less fortunate; using the coverage of an ideologically allied or controlled media, and labeling the opposition as opponents of change; and, declaring that any acceptance of the opposition's position is a step backward. This is done by labeling the opposition as enemies of progressive advancement. A recent example of this in recent times is a political ad in which a grandmother is thrown off a cliff. The ad produced by the Agenda Project in May, 2011, titled "Granny off the Cliff," supported the passage of "Obamacare" and was intended to create fear and distrust among the elderly, and to paint the opposition Republicans, led by Paul Ryan, Speaker of the House, as ruthless non-caring political leaders. As the video ran on TV there was no outspoken outrage by its proponents in President Obama's Administration as it supported their healthcare agenda.

With such strategies in the hands of the politically powerful, the challenge to the informed citizen becomes an even greater uphill struggle. Can an individual proclaim their beliefs when political power and the media are arrayed against him? How does the individual with limited resources compete? Today, it is far easier to avoid the informed change discussion rather than declare opposition to it, and in the process lose the battle in a marketplace of opinion where one's voice is muffled, and labeled, as heretical to the power agenda. Consequently, the idea of the singular independent voice is lost in the din of the day.

In this environment the ideas of freedom, morals and virtues are challenged by the broader society and the powerful. They would have you believe that freedom, morals and virtues are not individual possessions, but rather attributes shared by society; these behaviors are then defined, accepted and promoted as the new normal.

Today, as individuals, we struggle to define freedom. We translate freedom to mean that these are the actions of our personal will; to speak, to assemble, and to express opinion. To the contrary, freedom, morals and virtues are not singular possessions retained by the individual, but rather are defined, and exemplified, by our social interactions with others. Freedom is not declared by oneself, as in: "I am free!" Rather it is practiced and protected by individual moral acts towards others. To protect this freedom it must be preserved and advanced by the system of justice through the application of law, accepted and defined by previously established moral standards and acted upon by individuals through acts of fairness and justice.

Perhaps a better description of freedom is defined as:

1. The personal ability to act and choose as one may will, without causing harm to oneself and others.
2. The ability to advance oneself without a limitation imposed by others.
3. The contribution of one's efforts to the betterment of society.
4. Personal recognition, support, and protection of the freedoms and liberties of others.

5. Freedom is not a privilege defined by one group, and a prohibition imposed on others.
6. Freedom is a singular moral action taken by a single person towards another; it is not a social norm advanced by special interests or those in power.

15

MORALS

THE JUDEO-CHRISTIAN PARADIGM SHIFT.

In his Letter from the Birmingham Jail to the white ministers of Birmingham, Alabama, in 1963, Martin Luther King noted the differences between moral behavior—doing that which is just—and the accepted social norms of society. In it he argued the differences between justice and the established social norm; and, its consequence when society accepts and adopts restrictive social policies that separate individuals and communities. Martin Luther King defined the social norm as that which is "practiced, convenient and expedient in the individual." By preserving these commonly accepted norms they are legitimized; or perhaps better stated, they are the legalization of the socially accepted, and evolved, political culture. In this historical context it sustained and promoted racial segregation, imposing second-class citizenship on African Americans, and establishing, for the white majority, a clear privilege.

The white ministers in Birmingham accepted and supported the existing social construct rather than that which was required of moral and just behavior. It was an accommodation to the greater community's immoral behavior of institutionalized racism.

To be just is a matter of knowledge, such that knowing the good implies doing the good. Justice is a virtue practiced toward others; acting justly is the whole of virtue, not just part of it. Justice is achieved by understanding morals, acting morally, and carrying out its implied actions towards others, while acknowledging another's freedom and supporting it. Combined, these constitute just behavior. When applied, the good of the individual leads to the good of society and the advancement of the state.

Through the Judeo-Christian paradigm shift a new standard was established. It would no longer be the norms of society, but rather the establishment and application of morals that would guide societies. Morals established the new paradigm standard which changed the fundamental relationship between people. The standard, all people are equal, and all should be treated with love and dignity... always.

This shift transformed societies. No longer would the powerful, fear and traditions, reign supreme, but rather that individuals were equal regardless of era, tradition or location. And so it was that as nations rose and fell, old power and traditions faded and disappeared; but not the Judeo-Christian principles of love and caring. Supporting each other became the basis for all moral behavior. This moral standard is founded on the principle that individuals determine individual behavior, not society, nor the accepted social norm, nor the political order. This alternate interpretation and application is the *secular* idea. The principle behind morals is asymmetrical to the concept of power and cultural traditions which have their origins in dynastic thinking.

The moral principle established the clear expectation for

responsibility in interpersonal relationships versus the power of those in authority, or that of corrupt authorities founded on social tradition, power and fear. This principle is built upon the demand that individuals, who dignify, respect, protect and care for each other, produce a higher standard of living and advance society. Progress achieved and founded on knowledge through a shared understanding of acting justly.

This paradigm shift challenged the powerful, and established a new basis for justice and fairness. Furthermore, the Judeo-Christian faith shifted acceptable, behavior as previously defined by the powerful, to the preferred social interaction of the common man. If followed, no longer would the individual be subjected to the required behavior dictated by political leaders and the secular power; moral behavior would now be owned and acted upon personally regardless of location social constructs or traditions.

For the Jews, teaching morals began with the Mosaic Law—the Ten Commandments—which expressed the basic laws for the interaction between God and man, and man and man, all for the greater good of society. The fulfillment of Judeo-Christian philosophy culminates with the death and resurrection of Jesus Christ, reminding Christians of God's love for man, and by extension for each person to love his neighbor. Through the combination of these teachings modern western cultures sought to understand, and know, the moral equivalent of goodness and truth.

Morals are the standard that distinguish between right and wrong, and which are practiced everyday by people around the world, but can be, and often are, ignored in the expediency and heat of the moment. Morals may be described as those all-encompassing set of behaviors which all societies live by regardless of location; and practiced and applied by individuals in their interactions between themselves and others. They are the ultimate guideline for our social interaction, practiced by individuals, reaching beyond the self, and by extension, setting the standard for society as a whole.

The powerful may seek to ignore morals as they advance their power agendas by establishing new directions for their nation. However, the right and wrong of morals are immutable; they cannot be changed to fit a worldview, or a national agenda or cultural experience. What a powerful leader may demand within his borders is near impossible to extend beyond them, the North Korean experience.

The first part of this moral argument can best be described as:

What do I possess?

Morals can be defined in numerous ways, but perhaps in their simplest form they are the innate human abilities of intelligence (to think, analyze, evaluate, express, believe) and consciousness—differentiated thinking between right and wrong. Morals and thought are the innate attributes of man's character used in higher order thinking. These place the primary individual in a secondary position vis a vis the needs of others, and places our desires, appetites and ambitions below our intellect and consciousness. Through moral practice we attempt to know, and understand, life's dilemma, and attempt to discover the truth.

Understanding truth is more complex and centered upon the four ideas of: philosophy, religion, faith, and the countervailing motivated self-interest of the individual. Through philosophy we try to comprehend the relational and rational behavior of the individual in his interaction with society, and, at the same time, differentiating between the other three in order to understand their impacts. Plato, Socrates, and Aristotle explore these individualistic behaviors and described the outcomes through their arguments of rational thought, knowledge and understanding of individual human behavior. These ideas were juxtaposed against the need for the establishment of, and the functioning of, the state.

The Moral Imperative.

The second and equally important component of the moral question is: "If I am to be a moral person what must I do?"

This is easily answered through the following ideas: Each of us is born with the potential for *action* to do both good and bad. Goodness is a pursuit, whether through faith, intellect or our individual interaction with others—to treat others as we would want to be treated. This is known to us "the golden rule," or the law of reciprocity. And, through our actions we dignify others and support their efforts to be better persons. The second idea is reflected best by the Hippocratic Oath of *"do no harm"* to others or yourself. In my personal, and professional life, I must consider the impact of my actions on myself and others with whom I interact.

These two ideas—the ability to evaluate circumstance and the potential for action—impose the moral obligation on the individual to *dignify* others, to respect their ideas and persons, but to evaluate, their ideas and positions based on their merit. This requires that we apply our intelligence in the context of the first question of: "What knowledge and intelligence do I possess to analyze and evaluate the ideas presented?" Secondly, this serves to dignify those that speak, express informed ideas, and equally important, to defend, the defenseless against those that would do them harm. In this context we are not only obligated to offer agreement, if proper to do so, but to also take action through either the expression of alternatives or, in the act of "doing," when appropriate, that which addresses and advances the improvement of all. Through this cognitive analysis of the status quo and its alternatives we are obligated to provide assistance to those less fortunate, and to defend and resist when lives, ideas and freedoms are threatened by the ever present power of government and malevolence in society.

> *"Freedom consists not in doing what we like, but in having the right to do what we ought." Pope John Paul II*

The practice of moral behavior is individual, and the impact of moral behavior can only be diminished by the expansion of *accepted social norms—the socially accepted and motivated agenda* —which may, or may not, be moral, but maybe affirmed by social or political pressures. The application of these social norms is selective and applied to varying degrees given circumstance, options and alternatives, choices which are available to the individual at the point of discernment and decision.

Regardless of individual circumstance, beliefs or human condition, morals are applied throughout the human behavior hierarchy covering the entire span from survival through truth. Circumstance will determine their application, but what can be recognized is that when societies decline, or are governed by agendas, or, in the extreme, dictatorial power, the decline of moral behavior leads the way. The history of nations can be traced through the rise and fall of applied individual moral behavior, and the expansion of accepted social norms pushed by political, nationalistic, or expanding social pressures. The Roman Empire for example, and in modern times, Hitler's Germany, Stalin's Russia and Pol Pot's Cambodia, all cost millions their right to life.

Morals can be best expressed as virtuous acts of individuals towards others, and not the self. The following is a sample list of virtues or moral actions taken towards others.

1. Dignify those you meet and know.
2. Act with justice.
3. Do no harm.
4. The pursuit of individual excellence.
5. Courage.
6. Love and caring for another.
7. Honesty; no excuses.
8. Determination.
9. Forgiveness
10. Mercy

When we apply these ideas to the Internal Dialogue mode it is our internal thought that is the critical component which engages and directs our interactions, and it is in this concept that we apply our knowledge (education, discovery, opportunity, risk), principles, philosophy, and our pursuit of truth. However, when we begin to apply our thinking and actions we submit ourselves to a different set of conditions in response to the present circumstance. Additional variables enter into the process and influence our decisions: survival, social acceptability, philosophy, principles, and truth. To capture this revised construct it is easiest to describe it visually. It is then necessary to define the elements that apply to the logic of the model.

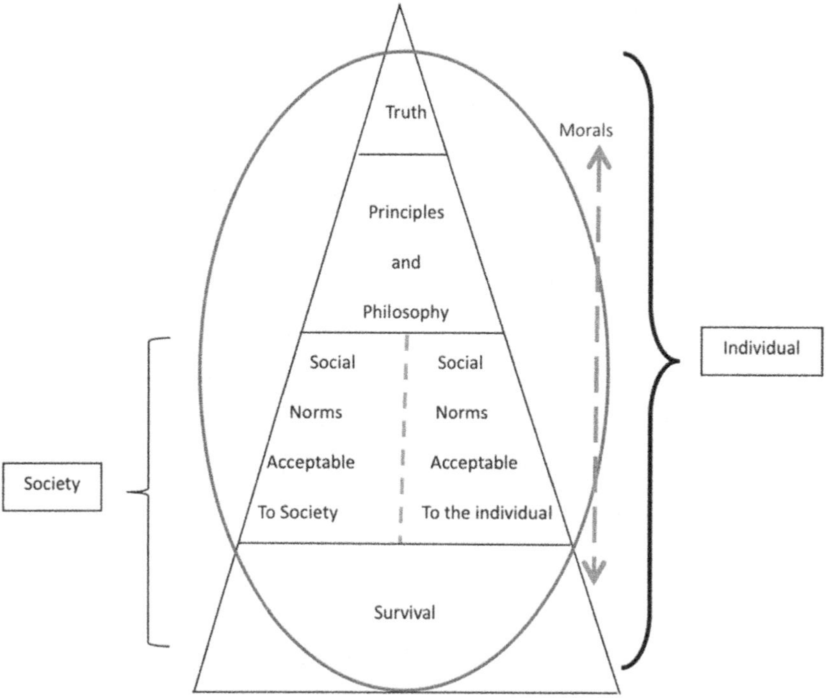

How we live and survive is a combination of all of these variables, each exerting influence and impacting our lives in a distinct manner.

. . .

Survival

How we survive is at the bottom of the diagram, it establishes our expectations and influences our initial motivations and determines how we live, and leads us to think in the most comprehensive ways. When we think of it in this context it forces us through both practice and thought to reach a higher self. Regardless of our economic conditions we are always trying to survive in the moment, always searching for the best opportunity and outcome. There are also those for whom survival is not only a condition of life but it is that part of every society around the world that struggles, every day given their limited opportunity. To survive requires seeking the best work opportunity, and it demands that we constantly learn if we choose to advance. For the poor, resources are limited, it is life in the moment, and the opportunistic physical labor, that produces today's income. Income derived from the physical labor that each person pursues, knowing that they can only do so much on any one day, with a limited skill set. The survivors' focus is the need to survive *today,* to earn enough money to meet *today's* demands, and if they are fortunate, to put something away for tomorrow.

And yet, within each of us it is the desire survive, to reach beyond, it is that which creates the push to be better off tomorrow than today by planting the desire to develop skills, knowledge, and the complimentary ability to do good. However, depending upon circumstance, our drive is impacted by the limitations and oppressions present in our lives and the market place. To survive demands that we be active in our pursuits and be receptive to any help that may be granted, regardless of source, if we are to achieve the better life.

. . .

Circumstance and Survival:

The Positive

- With opportunity we to seek to advance, to be better off tomorrow than today. And if we are willing to accept the related risk advance to better circumstances.
- In the absence of opportunity, and given present circumstance, the survivor's struggle can postpone any desire for long term planning and direction.
- If the political system is freedom based then the survival instinct leads to new opportunities, goals and efforts that support us to rise above the daily struggle, with the hope of achieving a better life. This drives skills-development and entrepreneurship (risk). The objective is to aspire to upward mobility in both the social and economic context.

The Negative

- If a nation is a young republic, the society will change and advance slowly as order, justice and freedom take root and self-governance learned. Knowledge of self-governance must be learned; it is not imbued in the human spirit, culture or in the establishment of government.
- However, if the need for survival is common, and reflects broad based frustration and desperation with the present political system and its leadership, it can lead to chaos, anarchy and revolution. Ultimately, a new and modified political order will be established replacing the

old, founded on the promise of satisfying the most basic of human needs, for the greatest number of people.

- Any broad based cultural or political change will not occur quickly, often condemning the individual to a life of struggles.
- A new political system may recognize the problems but it will require time to create solutions, or it may use fear to maintain power; and through force change the society to fit a new ideology and civil direction.
- The establishment of a new political order does not guarantee freedom.

16

SOCIAL NORMS:

THE RECOGNIZED REALITY OF THE THIRD GUIDING PRINCIPLE: EVOLUTION CHANGES EVERYTHING.

Before considering the issue of social norms it is essential to understand the application of the more commonly accepted idea of modern day norms and their creation, their application and impact on today's culture and society. Social norms are today's terminology for the old *mores* (commonly acquired customs and manners, social conventions and traditions). Today we divide our *mores* between the personal, our individual attitudes, perspectives and traditions, and, societal social norms; each with a different basis in context and behavioral outcome, and which may be practiced differently by segments of society and different cultures.

Mores

Societies, in general, live by what are accepted cultural behaviors developed by communities that broadly define their local and national culture, and which describe acceptable and non-acceptable behavior.

In today's culture the term *moral* has become synonymous with the acceptable mores and social norms or conventions, but they are not one and the same.

Mores are the acceptable social norms which constantly adjust, and evolve, to new common experiences, events, behaviors or social standards. Practiced *mores* expose indignity, identify previously unspoken wrongs, and expand our view of what is and isn't permissible. They redefine our acceptable individual behavior and establish the *cultural* right and wrong, and by extension, become the new expression of individuality; they are for example the "Me too" movement, the right to free speech, who has it—who doesn't, the freedom from religion push, the success and wealth debate, the Second Amendment argument, the Right to Choose versus Pro-Life, and the debate over the legalization of drugs. All are individual actions that define an internally focused personal expression of will, while creating a new national debate that redefines the limits of an old practice or the establishment of a new norm. It is the ability to do whatever one chooses, *if* the action is individual in its nature and victimless, then the practice, overtime, may be determined to be acceptable.

Social norms, by their very nature, have no impact on individuals unless illegal and prosecutable, but do impact our worldview and the immediate surrounding community; yet are considered personal choices by many and declared victimless.

The use of alcohol or illicit drugs are considered by many to be acceptable as they are deemed to only harm the user. However, neither drunk driving, nor the drug wars in Mexico, are victimless;

we declare them victimless because they may not touch us individually.

Human trafficking, the abuse of women and children, acts of violence that cause intentional harm, violence that supports the desire for power, or is reflected in the execution of power, honor killings, the punishment of the innocent. All remain *immoral* regardless of the society, location, political or religious precept.

These actions maybe cultural but all are immoral when applied to the question of right and wrong.

Morals, on the other hand, hold individuals to higher standards of behavior, and do not vary from culture to culture; their application remains beneficial regardless of location and tradition.

Applying the concepts:

- Mores are broad based common social values which are commonly accepted and built upon generational and cultural value systems.
- If social norms evolve over time, with no limits, then the morals within a culture or community are weakened in the process.
- Mores are supported by a broad, and diverse, mass media which may have no established standard of its own, nor adhere to their own moral precepts when determining output based on the preferences and consumption of the media's subscribers, viewers and readers, producing the ultimate business decision. This is a characteristic of the broad-based social media common to all informational sources. Media often

reports the news while trading on sympathy, sensationalism or revulsion; either attacking, attaching labels or supporting issues subject to their own interpretation of good or evil, as reflected in the attitudes of its consumer base, and its paying advertisers.

- The media accepts and advances the *change* agenda without an in-depth knowledge-based analysis, ultimately supporting the day's agenda, changing attitudes towards perceived commonplace social mores. This ignores the cultural challenges of society (the Chicago and inner city murder rates,) and other victimless crimes; behaviors which later become acceptable in an evolving, or matter of fact, society. It is only when extreme issues arise that the media declares indignation reflecting and aligning itself with common social revulsion.

"We live in a world of mass communication, where millions of people can be reached instantly with messages that are very polished, very attractive, and very urgent. As a result people do not hold on to the same idea for very long. Opinions are easily swayed, half-truths are easily believed, and worthless theories are easily embraced. ... at the very beginning of the information revolution the best information is seldom the latest information"

~Dale Ahlquist, The Complete Thinker

Discernment of the Social Norm

Individual Social Norm

Social norms are individual common and accepted social interactive practices within the greater community. These are in-the-moment responses to events and circumstance, performed in the present and which are essential to achieving our personal gratification as defined by our personal standards of behavior—our actions in response to peer and work pressures—and are behaviors which are defined as acceptable by the greater community.

Accepted Social Norms

As social norms evolve, and as certain behaviors become more commonplace, those which were previously unacceptable, gain acceptance.

These evolving revisions to the social norm either broaden or weaken the social and national fabric, and are most often responsible for changing society's moral attitudes.

Social change is constant, and any broad-based, accepted, behavioral change contributes to the advancement or decline of every society.

These changes don't occur quickly; rather attitudes require generational acceptance as older individuals may reject the change versus younger people who are more willing to accept it. In the process the taboo is lessened and modified and made acceptable, as the hubris of self-satisfaction is accepted over time.

As behaviors gain acceptance they cause a *pull* force on the status quo.

For those that oppose the new behavior an opposite *push-back* force is created, regardless of the perceived positive or negative impact of the change. These social forces have natural tensions built within them, and which can result in division and deep fracture lines within the social constructs of society. These, in turn, produce new agendas. For example, the high-income versus low-income social and political debates, racial tensions, religious versus secular beliefs, gay versus straight.

Regardless of this pull/push on the fabric of society morals are stretched and weakened as established social standards are relaxed and previously unaccepted behaviors become common place.

However, any desire or movement to restrict or accept change creates emotional social and political conflict. The seriousness of any activity is then considered in the context of the new trend—the revised norm—versus traditional practices, some behaviors become detrimental to the individual and society, and produce far reaching impacts well into the future.

17

THE RELUCTANT MODERATE VERSUS THE PROGRESSIVE ACTIVIST

The pull of progressive social and political change is constrained by the moderating forces within society. While recognizing social and political change, moderates may not benefit directly from new policies; nor do they necessarily subscribe to new ideas and trends. Moderates tend to be observers and not active participants; they watch and see the evolution of social change and government policies. While they are not direct participants in the movement they recognize it, and don't oppose it initially. They measure the need for opposition based on traditional values, religious or otherwise.

While acknowledging that social change and progressive policies are occurring, moderates won't readily accept the change agenda or its premise. They frequently view the change as a social fad or trend, and not as threats to their personal values. The moderate's response is defined by one of these four positions: (1) The trend is a temporary fad and it will pass. (2) I see the change happening and as I choose not to participate; it won't affect me now or into the future. (3) Does it matter? Will it change my life or community? (4) Will I have to pay for it? Will I become responsible for the choices others are making?

While moderates recognize the trends, the answer so often is, "it doesn't matter." And, as it doesn't matter, there is no need to engage in its opposition, preferring to defer resolution to the politicians and the courts. The issue remains out of their frame of reference and traditional thinking.

The moderate doesn't challenge the movement nor question its necessity; but rather sits on the sideline letting it play out. In the evolution of society the new behavior or social attitude has advanced, and is now part of the new accepted social norm and social fabric. At this point the movement is beyond the moderate's control, and the opportunity to influence the outcome has passed.

For moderates the issue is not to reject the evolutionary change out of hand, or actively embrace it, preferring to wait and see its effect—choosing not to accept, nor reject, it as it doesn't directly impact their wellbeing or community. Its impacts are considered to be the noise of fringe movements in society. However, over time, the evolutionary change becomes acceptable; the result of repeated social and media messaging. The opposition weakens and acceptance increases. The argument for it becomes: "Changing times requires changing attitudes."

The populace can be manipulated through the advocacy and promotion of a change agenda; the rationalized justification by special interest and the active alliance of a subscribing social, published and broadcast media, which may accept, advocate for, and promote the agenda.

. . .

The Political Outcome

Government sees change as a political opportunity created in the present, and into the future. This opportunity would be a system in which government redefines political alliances, identifies new recipients and beneficiaries, and promotes new acceptable social standards. Combined these actions leverage and motivate their political power base, effectively affirming the *exchange*—the promise of benefit for votes.

Those that seek social change create an environment in which behaviors are constantly challenged and redefined. Pressures challenge the pro or con of the previously accepted morals or *more* standard. When new social behaviors become politically acceptable and aligned with one party or another opposition rises and challenges are created, ultimately these behaviors may be affirmed or rejected through the judicial process. If confirmed, this new interpretation of behaviors produces political, judicial and social considerations which gain recognition and acceptance. This may ultimately include revisions to prior laws by legislative processes, including, but not limited to a laws redaction or rejected in its entirety as unconstitutional. In such cases a law's prohibition is removed, such was the case in Loving v Virginia where Loving was an interracial marriage, a prohibition by the State of Virginia. The Supreme Court's decision affirmed the right of the Loving's to marry and found that their rights, under the 14th Amendment, had been infringed upon by the state. The result is a redefinition or expansion of a right which is protected and advanced. This process expands the rights of the individual and the power of social movements, and which re-defines individual rights in law setting the new standard rather than the power of past social attitudes.

> *"Must the citizen ever for a moment, or in the least degree, resign his conscience to the legislator? Why has every man a conscience, then? I think that we should be men first, and subjects afterward. It is not desirable to cultivate a respect for the law, so much as for the right. The only obligation which I have a right to assume is to do at any time what I think right. It is truly enough said that a corporation has no conscience; but a corporation of conscientious men is a corporation with a conscience."*
>
> *~Henry David Thoreau, Civil Disobedience*

A social push arises when the desire for acceptance of any new behavior is pursued. For example, when a society deems that drug use is acceptable, or simply a matter of fact, then society will adjust, and laws will change, to accommodate the now common accepted behavior by reducing the perceived negative consequences. However, in the interim, a prediction can be made. For example, American marijuana use is expanding, supported by legal and non-legal growers in America and within the Mexican drug cartels. Groups fight for market share, money and access to users, with potentially grave, negative consequences to the active participants, and sometimes the sidelined non-participants. Today, marijuana is being considered for legalization by state governments, and if it is approved, will the state be able to capture a share of this new revenue source. States such as Colorado, Washington and California have jumped on this band wagon and are reaping new revenues which they will then decide how to spend out of political necessity, either in response to community needs, or as they seek to gain voter approval for their own decision making. In Denver, the city generated $29 million in additional sales tax revenue from Colorado's legalization of marijuana. (Carlos Illescas, The Denver Post, May 26, 2016)

Anticipated/Unanticipated Outcomes

- Subject to the level of participation in a particular behavior each community will determine if it is socially, economically, and politically beneficial to accept the new norm, transforming it to a government approved privilege, benefit or civil right.
- Laws are passed that reiterate, re-enforce, establish, or redefine the commonly accepted right and wrong. And through this process the *more* becomes the new standard, affirmed through the legislative process, resulting in a redefined cultural or social behavior.
- With the promise of new revenue political leaders will argue that there is an opportunity to create programs and benefits that address social deficiencies, with the promise that problems can be solved by the state only if the electorate approves a particular tax, candidate or party.
- Using the above politicians can support ideological arguments and segregate opponents of change creating social distrust and class warfare. The American Antifa movement's recent objection and protests to conservative speakers on The University of California, Berkeley, campus is an example of this social distrust.

The societal challenge is to question and judge the acceptability of any behavior.

When judicial processes are applied to previously non-accepted behaviors these social actions are judged against prior laws. Today, in America, solutions are sought in the courts and decisions made, which either reject or allow for the acceptance of new behaviors. If the courts accept the challenge and agree through judicial processes to review and approve the new behavior, they establish new rights and precedents into the body of law. With the change, reluctant or cheered acceptance by society will occur, the opposition will seek new ways to restrict the behavior, likewise new efforts will be undertaken that further affirm and authorize it. Social behaviors are evaluated against existing and prior benchmarks, and when laws are modified new standards of right and wrong are established. If rejected, the status quo remains.

- Social disunity will arise between liberals, moderates and conservatives, when this occurs politicians will respond to circumstance and opportunity with promises to protect society, advance wealth and position, and increase benefits to the community in an effort to retain power.
- The ludicrous: Even if based on health studies, governments do propose the ludicrous. For example, San Francisco attempted to place a law on the ballot that prevents circumcision (July 28, 2011). Government, in such cases, represents and responds to the voice of

special interests with the object of becoming the ultimate arbiter of right and wrong.

> *"An unjust law is a code that is out of harmony with the moral law. To put it in the terms of St. Thomas Aquinas: An unjust law is a human law that is not rooted in eternal law and natural law. Any law that uplifts human personality is just. Any law that degrades human personality is unjust."*
>
> *~Martin Luther King, a Letter from the Birmingham Jail, April 16, 1963*

Caution: Any accepted but unjust behavior defined as culturally or economically beneficial, supported by government or law, and which justifies an immoral act, does not change the outcome, nor make the wrong a right. An unjust law does not convert immorality into morality. Any law that reduces the value, capacity or capability of the individual, and is justified by social acceptance, does not change the morality of the issue. Although legal, the law remains unjust regardless of the government's desired intent or justification.

If, at the end of the day all is acceptable, then what isn't? *Morality declines.*

If the objective is to satisfy the greatest number of people accepting and legalizing new social norms will always be sought. In doing so, blame can be attributed to segments of the population;

the rich, a particular group, faith or another industry, for failure to support the change and advance. If society fails to correct the problem through the power of government, or if society permits the continued abuse, then extreme conditions are created. The idea of order and justice recedes, protests arise, and in the extreme, riots and chaos will follow.

Examples include the following:

1. Riots—limited social protest: recent modern day Greece
2. Chaos and Mob rule: The French Revolution
3. Political outcomes—controlling ideologies in which the individual becomes subservient to the government and individual freedom is lost, resulting in dictatorship or oligopolies in which all power is vested in the state.
4. Extreme versions of socialism include:

-Fascism

-Communism

-Theocracies

Next steps

Individuals and societies interact throughout all aspects of life. Our thinking engages the different elements of mores / social norms, principles and truth, as we respond to events, opportunity and risk. We make decisions and take actions that reflect our philosophical positions and rational thinking on the important issues of the day. And, how we respond is dependent upon our personal philosophies through which we align our priorities and interpret events and conditions. These will ultimately determine our social friendships and affiliations and political motivations. As individuals we often move between that which is acceptable based upon our desires, needs and circumstances, but rarely have the need to reach into the realm of principles and truth. Circumstances and events will determine which we use and apply based upon our immediate needs, desired satisfaction, and the moral behavior demanded.

To reach into the higher realm of truth requires a different type of thinking; principled and rational, these are the essence of who we are. People at these levels view the world through a different lens and are at times the most successful at innovation, creating change and speaking to the moral hazards of the day. They create wealth, not through the transactional wealth of Wall Street, but rather wealth built upon the creation of new ideas, goods and service. Bill Gates could not have created Microsoft if he did not apply basic math, science and organizational principles that drove the development of Microsoft. And, we hear Pope Francis and others speak of the need for stewardship of the earth and of the soul. We acknowledge the power of the individual but also recognize that the provision of an economic safety net is essential to the protection and recovery of individuals during times of duress and difficult economic circumstances.

And yet, morality, social stability and economic innovation (surprise,) are dependent upon the ideas of philosophy and truth; each essential to the advancement of any individual. To experience progress not only must these be present, but people must also possess social and economic stability supported by complimentary system of governance in which the individual is free to pursue success. The idea that a person need only be free to succeed is a fallacy; nations and people must possess, and have the necessary rights and know how, to self-govern. The mere existence of government does not necessarily grant and protect, nor advance, the essentials for a successful society. Nor does having a government, that promises all and delivers little, provide a great future for its citizens; a truth that isn't yet broadly recognized.

> *"Spontaneous order is self contradictory.* Spontaneity *connotes the ebullition of surprises. It is highly entropic and disorderly. It is entrepreneurial and complex.* Order *connotes predictability and equilibrium. It is what is* not *spontaneous. It includes moral codes, constitutional restraints, personal disciplines, educational integrity, predictable laws, reliable courts, stable money, trustworthy finance, strong families, dependable defense, and police powers."*
>
> *~George Gilder, Knowledge and Power*

Applied Individual Principles and Philosophy:

Our philosophies and principles reflect our efforts to reach our highest order thinking. They help us understand and interpret the world in which we live. They establish our moral and principled behavior; through them we make decisions and set the very direction of life. They help us:

- Establish our overarching pursuit of principles and truth.

- Determine and reflect the righteousness of our thinking and help us recognize the divisions in society.
- Establish the preferences and rules for the governing system.
- But, can be abused in the pursuit of individual ideology and power.
- They are the acts of principled and moral individuals, unwilling to accept as common behavior—the red line in the sand.
- They are the foundation for the ideas used to achieve truth.
- In the individual they can be used to justify good and evil.
- They are used as an argument in attempts to limit or redefine truth.
- Unrestrained principles and social philosophies can be used to change social thinking or used to achieve power.

Moral Discernment

As previously stated unlike mores and socially accepted norms, morals are immutable. Morals either are or are not, there isn't a middle ground, they can't be divided, adjusted or changed to fit circumstance. The sole consideration is of what is right or wrong, what is good or destructive of the natural law. There are no vagaries that exist between the two; morals are certain as they are universal truths, acted upon by informed individuals with clear understanding of right and wrong. Morals may best be described as the individual application of knowledge and principles in the pursuit of truth. There can be no individual moral, and a broader differentiated societal moral, determined and defined by cultural preferences and *norms*. However, *mores* are the common social behaviors that can change and evolve community to community, culture to culture, nation to nation.

Morals reflect the concept that each *individual* is unique, able to think and act solely, and impacts lives through his interactions with others. If a moral person acts morally and others act morally then a society by extension becomes a moral society. To achieve this requires a method of communication and knowledge of the expected moral behavior. This was previously done through the paradigm shift created by Judeo-Christian teachings, the practiced religious teachings that defined the right and wrong over the centuries. Jews and Christians may have been the earliest to define the moral standard of right and wrong, but the Greek philosophers also approached and attempted to define this question through their discussions on *ethos* (character) when they ascribed the rational behaviors of individuals.

However, when immoral behavior exists, a society degrades slowly, driven by the accepted *mores* of the day, perhaps eventually becoming immoral. Mores that apply to society as a whole are, by their very nature, a lesser standard than that which an individual may self-apply. However, there is no singular moral that applies to society as a whole and therein lies the challenge to any culture. Social norm conditions that transitioned are perhaps best reflected in the change in American attitudes as a result of the efforts of Martin Luther King in leading the protests of the Civil Rights movement, and Thurgood Marshall, who challenged the legality of such issues in the courts. They, in concert with many, transformed America's racial attitudes, creating and applying the moral standards of right and wrong to the broader racial discriminations in America.

Individually Applied Moral Determinations

- Personal guiding behaviors.
- Derived from moral teachings and beliefs and supported by individual principles, philosophy and a pursuit of truth.
- The common application of morals results in the greater social good.

Truth – The Ultimate Good

When we consider social norms, philosophies and principle we recognize that at the top of this hierarchy is truth. It is built upon these and is exhibited through acts of consciousness guided by a belief in the ultimate good, the pursuit of personal excellence, and God. There may be no mass truth, but there can be mass understanding of its roots, and thus, the basis for ideological, political and social change.

> *"A wise man will not leave the right to the mercy of chance, nor wish it to prevail through the power of the majority. There is but little virtue in the action of masses of men."*
>
> *~Henry David Thoreau, Civil Disobedience*

Truth demands an even higher plateau, one in which very few public figures have ever achieved. These are some of the few that changed the world and whose ideas survived political ideology, influence, and technological advancements: Moses and Jesus Christ, without them there would be no Judeo-Christian paradigm, Martin Luther King, Socrates, Plato, Mohammed and Confucius. Their ideas and teachings permeated the very roots of mankind, and established ideas which resulted in permanent change in morals, philosophies, cultures and societies. Each focused on change initiated within the individual, not the ideological change of society as a whole, but rather one person at a time.

Applied Truth

- Creates change by appealing to the highest individual ordered thinking.
- Is rational in its pursuit of the ultimate good.
- Requires the individual to apply it in a singular/individual mode.
- Extends the ultimate good through action.
- Lives by the standards demanded of the ultimate good.
- Is acted upon individually; it is the broadest of rules that can affect society, but cannot be applied across the entirety of the social spectrum by a single action.
- Creates change by affecting the social norms of society as a whole.
- Cannot be used for control or power.

- Truth creates change within individuals; independent behavior evolves which may not be accepted or understood, and which may be rejected given its potential consequences.
- Individuals act regardless of personal cost or consequence, they assume and accept the related risk.
- Establishes an understanding of the nature of man, the spirit of man, the perfection of the spirit, and the comprehension and belief in God.

A society can be truth-based when men and women of conscience are involved. Consider the American Declaration of Independence in which Thomas Jefferson proclaimed America's singular guiding principle: "*Life, liberty and the pursuit of happiness*," not as a society, but as the pursuit of individual success, the advancement of the human spirit, and through that expression of freedom comes the advancement and changes necessary within society. It is the pursuit of individual development, and it reaches beyond the self to the greater community.

Jefferson never believed that it would be the power of government that could, or would, create change, but rather the individual acting in his own right, applying his own individual *pursuit of happiness* that would change society, and not the emotion or demand for individual entitlement, and creation of equality, which was the Marxist or French Revolution re-definition.

Through this understanding of happiness, it established and affirmed the Constitution's idea that power resides in, and is derived from, the people. This concept forces the individual to be responsible for the self, to act morally, and to pursue each individual's self-defined idea of happiness—the ultimate pursuit of principles, philosophy, and truth which ultimately define our individual purpose.

However, this very idea of individual excellence exists in conflict within society as the state, which advances and promotes the general welfare, never seeks the ultimate good, but pursues that which creates the greatest benefit, the commonly accepted good. In this pursuit then, society never seeks the highest standard, but strives for that which creates the greatest emotional happiness (joy), or the best socialized, common solution for the greatest number of people. In the process principles, philosophy, morality and truth are minimized in order to provide the greatest benefit rather than the greatest good. And yet, it's the very pursuit of truth which creates the greatest change within society; it is the very idea that in order to practice and pursue this, the individual must be free, and, to be free, requires that the political system support and provide the requisite individual freedom.

When morals are practiced and truth is known the individual discovers a new self, explained by the greatest definitions and application of the term, liberated. To be liberated transforms the individual cognitively, but it also forces us to recognize that true freedom, while providing the peace of understanding, also challenges the individual *to do,* at which point the prior definition of freedom is brought to the forefront, requiring the individual to act, not only out of self-interest but in the interest of others and the greater society. The result is an individual acting in a fully integrated manner through knowledge, principle, philosophy and truth, and through this freedom preserving the individual *rights of man* through personal risk and action against the rationalized justification, or social agenda, of special interests, and the power of the state. "To do" requires the individual to speak out, and to challenge the actions of the powerful through their own knowledge and applied personal power.

> *"The world has never had a good definition of the word liberty, and the American people, just now, are much in want of one. We all declare for liberty; but in using the same word we do not all mean the same thing. With some the word liberty may mean for each man to do as he pleases with himself, and the product of his labor; while with others the same word may mean for some men to do as they please with other men, and the product of other men's labor. Here are two, not only different, but incompatible things, called by the same name – liberty. And it follows that each of the things is, by the respective parties, called by two different and incompatible names – liberty and tyranny."*
>
> *~Abraham Lincoln, Sanitary Commission Fair, Baltimore, April 18, 1864.*

When one considers these ideas a new political order is revealed, and can be constructed recognizing the social and political needs of man. This concept is reflected in the following diagram:

Pursuit of Truth

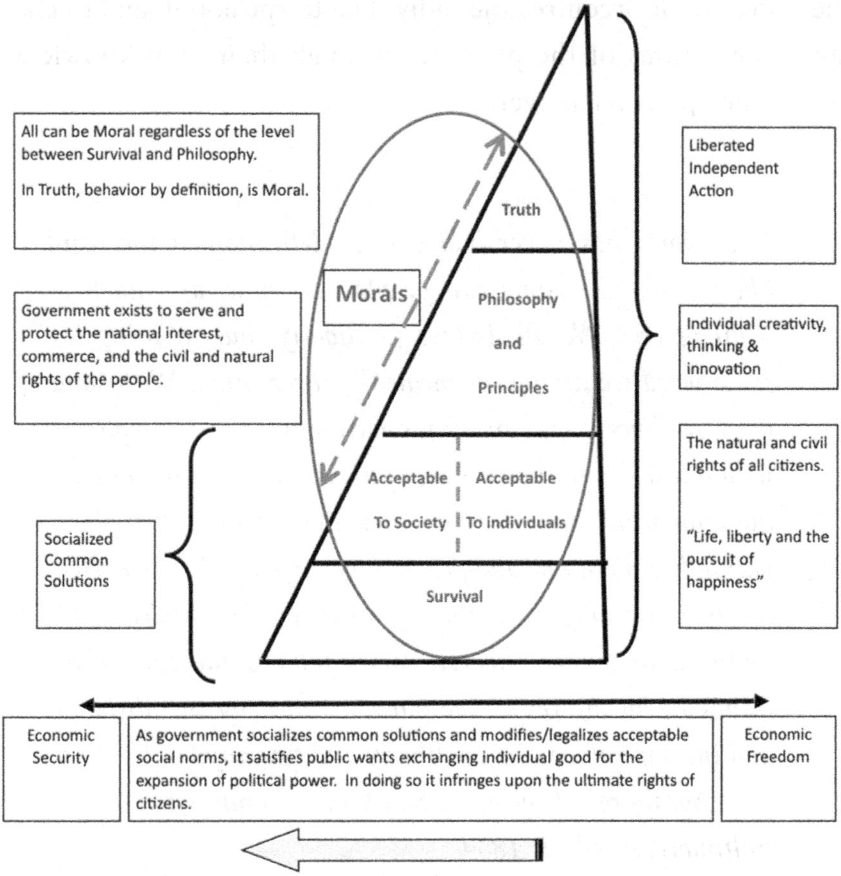

18

MY PURPOSE

THE ABILITY TO CREATE CHANGE

When liberty is considered in the context of the pursuit of truth, and when its elements are combined with knowledge and risk, the ability to create change is established. Liberty is the final element which permits individuals, and, by extension, society to create the greater political, social and economic changes that advance nations. It is the application of our human effort and internal drive which creates, and changes, the very condition of man. It is our deepest understanding of our intellectual capital and the exercise of our individual freedom which produces excellence, moral behavior and innovation; and, it is in exercising these, in their appropriate and combined context, which enables us to create the greatest potential for progress in all its forms.

In a republic, the power of ideas and freedom evolves and changes the individual, impacting all aspects of life—their social, economic and political circumstances. Ingrained in this desire for freedom is also the desire for survival, self-satisfaction and power.

It is this desire which seeks alternative means. For many systems throughout the world, the preferred method to achieve this is the promise and re-interpretation of social paradigms and the expansion of social programs.

Republics begin with the idea of a representative government which exists to protect the greater societal good. But, when overreach occurs, the government, not the people, becomes the final arbiter of behavior, proposing both the solutions to society's problems, and the necessary approvals for a paradigm shift, which can be either positive or negative. It is these actions which have the potential to stall, or destroy, our most fundamental social constructs.

Republics are slow to change as politicians and political leader's trade on their appeal to the broadest constituencies, reminding voters of their past efforts to deliver on their wants and actions of the issues of the day. In the process they advance their own name and ideology. With name recognition and office comes power and opportunity, but not necessarily effective and knowledgeable leadership; a condition endemic to republics and perhaps the greatest blessing for preserving and protecting the rights of its citizens. Incompetence, ignorance, and radical thinking, can have a home in politics, however, trading on rhetoric and promises without effective solutions always produces a negative consequence.

To retain or gain office candidates must appeal to the broadest electorate. This process is affirmed at the voting booth, and ends with voter expectations that their newly empowered candidates will deliver on their promise(s). Through the political provision of benefits, government has the potential to erase the very principles on which a republic was founded, reducing its guiding principle of freedom to the idea of *"equality."* And, in the process the original purpose of *to serve* is transformed, substituting *to serve* with *to provide,* that which the individual, given present circumstance and risk, is unable or unwilling to provide, and wherein the individual —the voter— becomes the beneficiary.

Power, once established, flows from the permanence of the office; confirmed through the constitutionally defined re-election process. Drastic change, unless supported by broad social movements and political leadership (presidential politics in America), is slow and limited given the divisive nature of the legislative process and the moderating effect of the electorate. It is this competitive electoral process that creates political stability and future change as political leaders respond to the needs and wants of voters, but only after negotiation and consensus is reached. Herein lies the strength of the republic; nothing occurs without political and social approval and resistance, and when great political achievement does occur, voters will decide to approve or reject the new direction in the next election. We have seen this throughout the history of republics; as societies advance the actions of their leaders affects their nation's development, not in great leaps forward, but through slow and methodical political argument.

Can a community prosper when market and risk related opportunities are limited? Government programs are created to provide many forms of benefit based on the idea that the poorest of society should share in the benefits created by a rich nation. To achieve this, the concept of a state funded and managed *social justice* was invoked to address poverty; a system which may not have been necessary, but was beneficial given the conditions created by limited opportunities in the market economy. In such communities, and to sustain stability, the state becomes the source of added financial support, and may become the long term income assistant if market conditions don't improve. In the process it also establishes a form of economic segregation founded on reduced expectations, but which sustains the livelihood of the community.

National debt and taxation become the means to satisfy the electorate in pursuit of the idea of income security and equality of person-hood, paid for by debt and through new taxes. The challenge is defining and designing safety net programs which address specific problems, while limiting their application and providing the motivation to risk. However, caution must be taken to recognize that the desired satisfaction of social needs leads to ever increasing social program expenditures, a burden which may not be sustainable, but is granted as a result of political promises and demands: the Greek experience.

Institutional movement, bureaucracies, or political evolution follows the trends established by prior administrations, and do not attempt drastic change as it disrupts and threatens established power, rather they hold to the very promises made in prior campaigns. Promises are linked to either individual beliefs, or the promise of benefits to constituents, which voters will either accept or reject.

Leadership and Truth

Republics rely on compromise rather than dictate, creating social and economic solutions through a political process which can either produce positive outcomes or failure of action. Inaction preserves the status quo of power, and avoids related political risk. Proposing change in the status quo is a risk many politicians are unwilling to take as failure becomes evident on bigger issues; safe issues are then the means to a long political life. The challenge for any republic lies in combining political leadership with principle, not ideology, to not only lead, but to address the changes which society needs to advance without imposing undue economic burden on the tax payer or the economy. And, where politicians fear to venture, purposeful citizens gladly accept the risk and the challenge of creating change.

> *"Informed common sense is the means of evolution of higher levels of intelligence, civilization and social organization, from primitive self-authorized "gangster" systems of governmental and tyrannical subjugation and exploitation of defenseless, unorganized people, toward more sympathetic cooperative culture of equality of legal rights and privileges and of self-determination. The most understanding of humanitarian philosophies of history have been thought out by men with deep sympathetic natures who have experienced bitter suffering with their people under the yoke of legalized privilege and injustice."*
>
> *~Edward J. Kempf, Member of the Wisconsin State Assembly*

However, in a fear society the power to create is limited and controlled, which is essential to the survival of the political order, and maintained through the exercise of power over the individual. As a consequence, totalitarian regimes are relatively short-lived unless supported by the opportunities created by external and uncontrolled events as they rely upon the individual strength and character of the dictator. Can North Korea survive without the support of China? Dictatorships begin to fail as leaders age and the competition for succession begins. The dictator will pass the power on to a selected successor, however, in time, that too will fail, created by the impact of global events and change, as demonstrated by North Korea's recent attempts to negotiate a new relationship with America.

Ultimately, a national collapse becomes inevitable unless change is created by the new order; if a collapse occurs then the nation or society is forced to rebuild and evolve. Often the new order will appear to be different, but will act and rule similarly to the prior order. The new rulers promise an improved quality of life and opportunity; in reality they are simply moving the chairs on the *Titanic,* producing nothing more than symbolic modernization, a promoted image of change without real results. It becomes the same structure with a different label. An example of this is the former Soviet Union, perhaps the most recent and most recognized failed state in recent history, collapsing from within and replaced by a system of governance, and a new Russian Constitution, but with *all* power held in the hands of Vladimir Putin.

Change?

Previously, in the pursuit of truth, the top of the pyramid was titled simply "Truth." Individuals at this level ignore the politics of the day and focus on the essential belief of man's purpose. To achieve this level, a single man or woman is willing to accept undefined, and unknown, personal and political risk. Through direct involvement, and the ability to communicate and lead, they change the world. Focused on the prevailing conditions or problems, they question the status quo and apply principles to re-direct the accepted *common-think.* In the process they establish and apply the basic standard of what is just, rather than the accepted social norms. They directly impact society by challenging political ideologies and by placing the individual, once again, at the center. If successful in their endeavor progress is advanced. These few players are the game changers.

This *truth* position is opposed by the power structure as it implies that change is necessary and desired. Truth, by its very nature, implies that the pursuit of a higher standard of social behavior is required if society is to advance. However, given the rarity and uniqueness of truth-leaders, it is only when great wrongs are in need of correcting that such individuals rise to the task, pushing against the entrenched power and social agendas to create change. Progress, in real political terms, rarely happens quickly, as empowered political leadership is slow to evolve. In the process, social demands are deferred, the moral question ignored and the permanence of elected power preserved.

In a creeping society, such as America, the great wrongs have been addressed. Today the questions revolve around the concept of social equality and moral position, approved or rejected by government decision. And, by the very nature of the decision, it impacts the interactions between people, and between people and their government. It redefines what is acceptable, and the role of the citizen and transforms the social contract.

The question of change reaches beyond its definition, and, to fully understand change and its sources, we must first consider its impact. In a free society change comes from two distinct sources: *acquired knowledge* and *truth.* Societies are changed by the very effects of these two forces. For example, through applied knowledge we have seen dramatic advancements in technology. People such as Thomas Edison, the Wright brothers, Bill Gates, Steve Jobs and Mark Zuckerberg, have transformed the market economy. These men are in contrast to the truth-leaders such as John Locke, Thomas Jefferson, Jesus Christ, and Martin Luther King, who changed the understanding of man and his relationship to each other, and the purpose of government, each impacting the very nature of society. Each leader hit the three circles in the center of the overlap area, impacting every part of the culture, the economy and the nation, and, in the process, creating great permanent change.

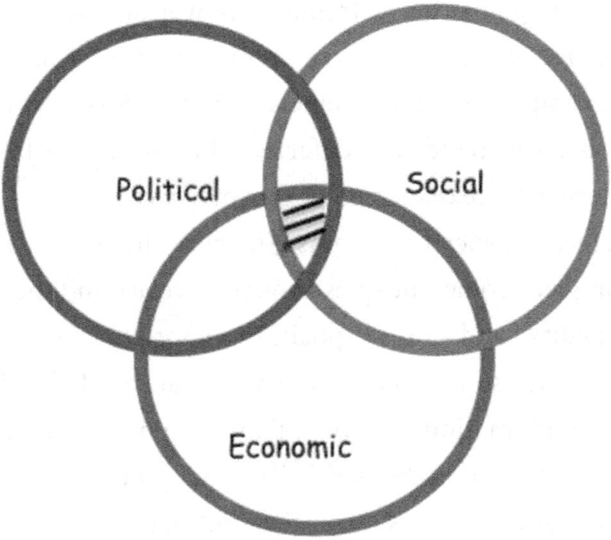

19

FREEDOM'S PURSUIT

INTEGRATING THE DIFFERENT FORCES

It is the exercise of life with its daily tasks and routines which dominate our actions and reactions. We rarely apply our greatest knowledge, as our lives are not typically filled with crises or fears. If blessed with a good life these challenges do not occur every day, but if we live in *survival mode,* every day has its challenges. We reserve our deepest thinking to the consideration of bigger problems and newly presented opportunities; how to proceed, how to answer, and how to react to those issues which deeply affect our lives? We evaluate our position though our education and experience, seeking to make the right decision, rather than simply reacting to it. We build up our war chest of knowledge to do battle with whatever issue arises, finding the best solution for us after thoughtful consideration. Addressing issues, seeking opportunity or solving complex problems, regardless, our minds are always working. Our actions are dictated by our response to opportunity with each action differentiated by the routines of the day and the complexity of the problem; regardless of the topic we think through the problem to find, and make, effective decisions while minimizing the corresponding risk.

We attempt to apply rational thought considering all aspects of our decision making while applying it to work, family, community and nation. We think in social, economic and political terms, evaluating our interactions with friends and co-workers while observing the positive and negative of the interactions, and we measure and judge it all against our personal moral standard.

We either live in a free society or a fear society, subject to the order, freedom and justice in place, reacting to the power of leadership's direction and its ultimate impact on our individual lives. We consider it all in the context of our freedom or fears, and the income and opportunities it affords us. We seek progress and change for the better, for if we are to succeed we must remain independent and avoid submission to the acceptance and reduction of *group think*; the malaise and *feel good* of every society.

To apply and understand our thinking, previously discussed concepts are combined to show their interaction, and the desired goal of achieving individual purpose and progress. The following graphic maps the concepts demonstrating the relationship between acquired knowledge, risk and competition, individual power and truth, and its resulting impact on purpose and progress, the overlap between the social, political and economic environments.

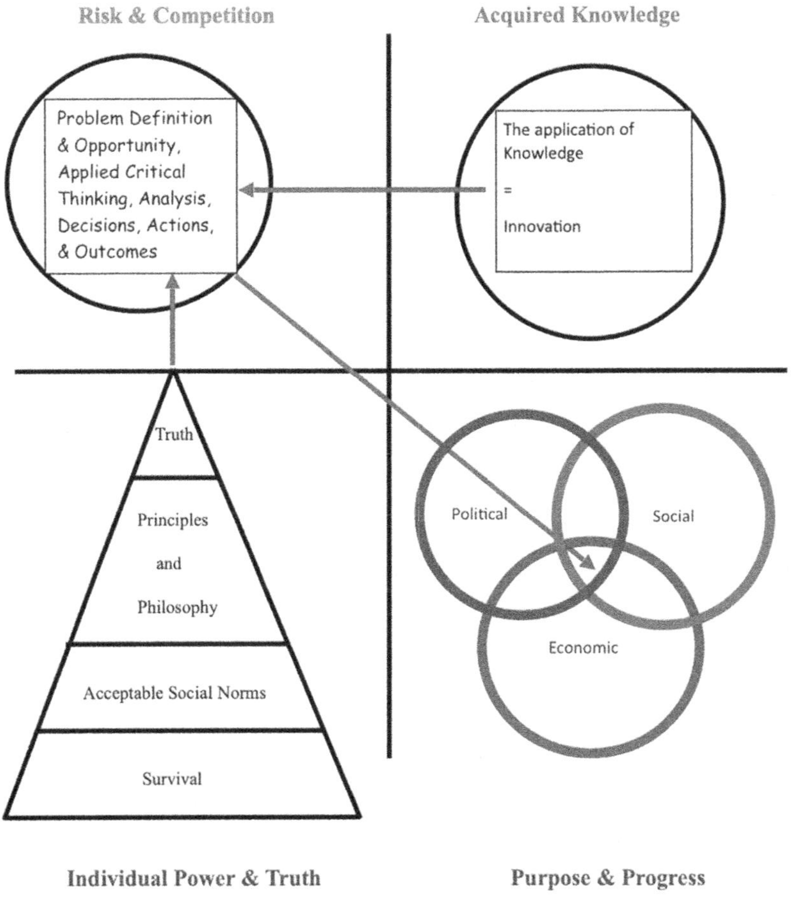

What is required to hit the Change/Progress impact zone?

The impact zone is the very heart of the three circles, not the general overlap between two circles, as that remains temporary in its purpose, intent and execution. Permanent change is derived through the combination of risk, acquired knowledge, and individual power and truth. When these are combined, social and technological advancements follow. The pursuit derives from man's innate desire for freedom, and his ability to discover and to create solutions to problems. So strong is the drive that freedom takes on a life of its own, pushing man to discover, to achieve, and to transform the status quo. In the process, the pursuit of freedom creates its own motivation for human achievement, establishing new standards that define culture, humanity and creativity.

The sole application of morals, principles and philosophy is unable to create change directly, as these are personal behaviors and are difficult to translate into broad social ideas and constructs. Rather, they are executed individually, one act at a time, between two people. As individual behaviors these will always be challenged by the opposing forces of the accepted social norm with the desire to preserve the status quo. Thus, the ability to create change is slowed within the community, especially when opposed by moderates and existing power structures. Rarely, if ever, will a single person practicing philosophy or principle be willing to risk all for change. Likewise, the person who isolates himself with the idea that he is dedicated to the pursuit of his contemplations is, or may be unwilling, to leave the certainty of his position as this entails risk. Consider a man in his self-imposed isolation; if not supported by someone else at some point he must exit his isolation simply to seek food and sustenance, in the process incurring risk. Likewise in the pursuit of freedom, man must be willing to take risk in order to change conditions, and the person most likely to practice truth is the one that is most likely, and willing, to risk all.

Like the truth-seeker, the innovator is also able to hit the center of the three circles and create permanent change. However, unlike the truth-seeker, the innovator risks only his—or another's—money, which may, over time, produce successes or failures if the market rejects the ideas and products. The application of principles and philosophy from an individual and leadership perspective, becomes ever more relevant to the leader as the challenge of success becomes more critical to the success of the business. With no guarantee, the challenge is how to deal with the everyday crises of the business; principles and philosophy will determine how well, or poorly, success and pressures are handled.

In today's society, achieving great societal and political change is difficult, and hitting the center of the three circles even more so. Progress then, only occurs when the pursuit of truth and the application of risk and knowledge are applied in a combined fashion to achieve our individual power and purpose.

Freedom is the combination of these factors which allows us to seek our own individual change and success; they provide the balance in our lives which leads to the exercise of our individual humanity, and which sustains our drive for survival and success. In practice this is extraordinarily difficult to achieve as we are continuously challenged by life and its daily struggles, compounded by our effort to achieve excellence. All of these may be ongoing and conflicted at the same time.

Pope John Paul II spoke of the essence of humanity in his book *Crossing the Threshold of Hope,* and the ultimate journey in the pursuit of truth and understanding. Our pursuit of freedom is the result of our acts of conscience, our treatment of others, knowledge, risk, independence, responsibility; all produce the desire to take risk that encourages us to act against those forces that would deprive us of our independence and purpose.

"True freedom is not advanced in the permissive society, which confuses freedom with license to do anything whatever and which in the name of freedom proclaims a kind of general amorality. It is a caricature of

freedom to claim that people are free to organize their lives with no reference to moral values, and to say that society does not have to ensure the protection and advancement of ethical values. Such an attitude is destructive of freedom and peace."

Pope John Paul II

However, it is only through the power of individual purpose (the combined result of knowledge, risk, and the pursuit of truth), that a person impacts and creates permanent social change; it is the application of thought and reason, and the use of each individual's intellectual capital that achieves this change.

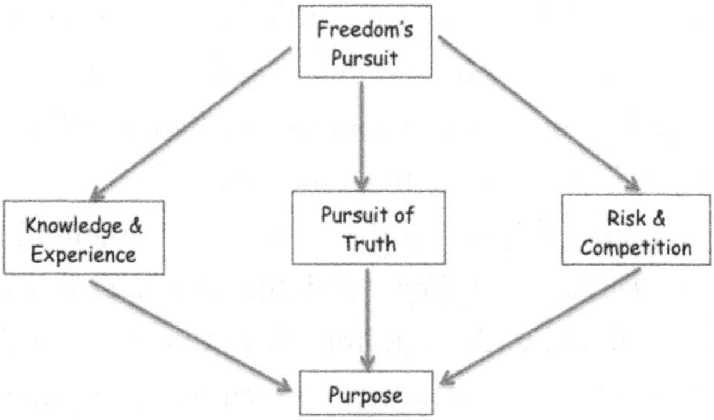

Other social change can come from a drastic and sudden change in circumstance, the desire for social and political revolution for example. Ideology and leadership then redefine the new social construct and power structure. If the revolution is led by men and women with a vision of social and economic freedom, and if the desire is to protect that vision through constitutional means, then the outcome can be beneficial, albeit not guaranteed. In fear-societies people will revolt against the existing order, or it may collapse under its own failings, as new leaders speak of new beginnings and adopt new philosophies, promising a new era of human equality. For example, Hugo Chavez and Nicolas Maduro, who bankrupted Venezuela and starved its people. As in so many instances, the previous power structures return under new management, and a new fear society ultimately recreated. The success or loss of that opportunity for real freedom and opportunity will be dependent upon the actions of the individuals engaged in leadership's power. If the opportunity for change is wasted, then the advancement of society and the individual is lost.

For me, my view of the world requires the understanding of all of these elements with the recognition that change is only achieved through the full comprehension of circumstance, and the role of responsibility in the individual. If not protected, the loss of individual liberty and identity is a possibility; the consequence of which is unlimited and unrestrained political and economic power leveraged against the individual. To protect against this potential outcome it is my obligation—not right nor privilege—to pursue knowledge, and an understanding of the conditions and circumstances to which I am exposed, and to be prepared to oppose those that would threaten my individual right to create, think, risk and act as I see best.

This stands in contrast to the social norms concept of the *worldview* which exists at the lowest positions on the "Pursuit of Truth" hierarchy, and which entails the granting of personal power to others in exchange for personal benefit, social acceptance and recognition. This end state has the least beneficial impact for the nation's future and creates the greatest liability and impact on the individual; the establishment of unrestrained growth of governmental power supported by group-think, and providing the least long-term motivation or benefit to the citizen and society.

One final idea: Our desire for freedom comes from the singular recognition that our individual success is the result of our internal drive to pursue personal achievement, built upon knowledge, risk and the pursuit of truth. Only in understanding, accepting and applying these concepts can I remain free.

ADDENDUM

To further explain this *Freedom's Pursuit* and these fundamental ideas in the broadest context—and in their application to our social interactions; how they affect our economic success; and, how we interpret our political world—five (5) simple guiding principles were developed to evaluate our complex world, one comprised of varying cultures, economies and political systems. By applying these principles I could evaluate the conditions that affect all people and reason the probability of success or failure, or to their detriment, the outcome created by sustaining the status quo. These five principles are:

1. Knowledge is the key to success

Individuals solely possess knowledge and societies can only advance when individuals pursue the development of their own intellect. Access to knowledge may be considered a natural right but it requires that societies act to establish the method by which it can be pursued and achieved; to not do so relegates the individual and society to fewer opportunities. Social and political processes will determine which methodologies will be developed and will vary in their establishment and execution; regardless, improving the human condition is an obligation held by all if the destitute and their conditions are to be improved. Global competition will further decide which methodologies work best as freedom's pursuit will be the ultimate judge of the most effective systems. These are broad principles, the first critical to measure the ability for a society to advance. Without education how does a society advance?

2. Innovation destroys the status quo

The application of intellect affects every endeavor undertaken by man, it is individually owned and applied, and is risk based, whether it is technical, scientific or simply the daily application of work. Every discovery and application of intellect and risk results in new ideas and practices producing an expansion of individual and corporate intellectual capital and property. Innovation is the ultimate driver for the advancement and economic well-being of societies as innovation is global, its deployment is unfettered by language, borders or government control.

3. Evolution changes everything

Societies change because the larger world evolves and changes. For example, the America's Civil Rights movement was essential to the change that took root in the South. Whether by intent or not societies evolve, and, any effort to limit or restrict change will not succeed resulting in internal conflict—in the worst case scenario civil wars. It is far better for individuals and nations to accept change as promoted by moral behavior and knowledge. Knowledge, a standard is essential for the greater good; a standard which reaches beyond ones-self to establish and preserve individual rights but which can always be perverted by powerful movements. To argue against change is an attempt to preserve the status quo and the retention of the present power. To be successful all change must begin with the preservation and recognition of individual rights. The necessary caution: This is a broad principle, the first to measure a society's ability to advance.

4. Injustice creates oppression

Governance in one form or another is no more than the methodology which brings order to societies; it is the contract which we enter into and grant through our consent, objection or acquiescence to the greater local will and national power. Justice defines our acceptable behaviors, regulates and controls our economies, and controls the application of our knowledge and choices. Martin Luther King perhaps said it best in his *Letter from the Birmingham Jail* to the white ministers of Birmingham in which he explained that any government can pass legal laws consistent with their own rule. The questions he challenged the Birmingham ministers include: Are these laws moral? Do these laws enhance and protect the individual? Or do they remove opportunity and, by design, create a citizen with less standing under the eyes of the law? If so, did the government—and through its laws and practices —reduce the equality and equal opportunity of citizens, and by extension create oppression?

. . .

5. Truth is knowledge and understanding

The four prior rules strive to create the ultimate understanding of what it takes to be free. However, to understand our own personal pursuits we must acknowledge the role *truth* plays in each person's endeavor to define his or her own purpose; and, through the application of this purpose pursue their own life journey to achieve their dreams. Furthermore, it is important to recognize that truth is not "what I want to believe." If this is the case then societies will fail and progress will not be achieved as individuals define their own ideological beliefs and not what is acceptable to others. Truth begins with the moral standard of respecting and doing for the other that which is best; a standard that places the other ahead of the one. This idea is the most difficult to achieve socially. It is not an exchange or a trade driven for the benefit of an agenda; it is the gift that preserves freedom.

The Cautionary Rule:

Ignorance is the domain of the uniformed and inexperienced.

This is a simple rule that can easily precede the prior five. However, if we fail to apply our knowledge and intelligence, we defer our essential thinking and analysis to those that would gladly take it from us—a result of our decided inaction. It is here that the application of political power grounded in the actions of individuals, institutions and governments deprive the citizen of his/her basic rights.

. . .

The Sherwood Rule:

Past performance is a predictor of future results.

This is an idea provided by my good friend, Rand Sherwood. We can apply this idea of past performance and future results to our individual actions as well as to leadership, whether corporate or political in its nature. If we accept that which has occurred in the past, and don't challenge nor consider its impacts in the present, then we declare our intent to accept its future consequence as a non-changing, non-advancing future bereft of opportunity.

Made in the USA
Monee, IL
04 November 2026

67383859R00154